Reading Tests in the Classroom: an introduction

Denis Vincent

NFER-NELSON

Published by the NFER-NELSON Publishing Company Ltd.,
Darville House, 2 Oxford Road East,
Windsor, Berkshire SL4 1DF

First Published 1985
© Denis Vincent
ISBN 0-7005-0563-6
Code 8156 02 1

Photoset by David John (Services) Ltd, Maidenhead
Printed by Billing & Sons Ltd, Worcester

Distributed in the USA by Taylor & Francis, Inc.,
242 Cherry Street, Philadelphia. PA 19106–1906. USA.

W 28286 £5 95. 12.85

Reading Tests in the Classroom

CONTENTS

Introduction

This book is intended as a 'primer' on the testing of reading. It has been written for the teacher of reading who requires a basic introduction to a subject which, in some aspects, has a technical mystique associated with it.

It would seem that many teachers teach reading more effectively than they test, assess or evaluate it. This, at least, is a reasonable conclusion to draw from the findings of a major research project which were reported while this book was still in draft form. This project, Evaluation of Testing in Schools Project (ETSP), was funded by the Social Science Research Council to investigate a range of questions in the field of educational assessment. The report in question, *Testing Children*, by Gipps, Steadman, Blackstone and Stierer (1983), raises concerns over both the quality of tests used in schools and the way they are used and interpreted. This research dealt with educational testing in general but it is evident that reading tests are particularly widely used by both LEAs and schools and the findings apply with particular emphasis to reading. Some of the following chapters refer to specific findings of the ETSP research and the report makes useful – and sometimes salutory – further reading by which many teachers might evaluate their own use of reading tests.

The problem of quality in reading tests raised by ETSP is tackled in detail in a companion volume to this book – *A Review of Reading Tests* (Vincent, Green, Francis and Powney, 1983). This is a series of descriptive and critical reviews of published reading tests currently available in the UK. *A Review of Reading Tests* thus provides initial information about what tests are available – a need also noted by ETSP – and some guidance over the problem of 'Which reading test?'. Inevitably, an introduction to reading tests, such as this book, needs to make reference to examples. However, as the majority of tests mentioned are fully described and referenced in the companion volume the inforation is not, for the most part, repeated here. The reader requiring amplification is advised to examine the associated review or – if possible – to refer to actual copies of the test materials themselves.

This book deals with a second set of problems – the use and interpretation of reading tests. The account has been kept as simple as possible with a minimum amount of reference to statistical material. Purists may well feel that this has resulted in some oversimplification. However, it is easy for those who are statistically-minded to underestimate the newcomer's need for the subject to be introduced in gentle and small doses. The intention has been to sensitize the teacher of reading to the statistical aspects of assessment, not to write yet another statistics text–book. Study of such a source would be a *second stage* of a programme of learning of which only the *first stage* is attempted in this book. Where appropriate, the reader is referred to slightly more advanced accounts for further reading.

The decision to concentrate upon reading rather than upon the general assessment of language needs some explanation. In part it might be defended on the grounds that many teachers place a higher premium upon developing reading than upon written or oral communication and that the greatest current perceived need for assessment is therefore in reading. This is not entirely convincing and assumes that 'what is, ought to be.' It would be fairer to argue that as a language skill reading is different in kind from speaking and listening or writing and that an altogether different type of discussion would have been required to introduce assessment in these areas. They present different, as well as greater, problems. There have certainly been fewer practical advances in the assessment of these areas – either through lack of professional interest or the intractable nature of the task. It may be necessary to accept that while teachers and researchers can strive for greater understanding of children's spoken and written language, these modes are never likely to be assessed as conveniently as reading.

The first six chapters of this book concentrate upon the standardized reading test and its uses. Chapter 1 reviews some of the main characteristics of reading tests and considers some of the principal features by which they can be differentiated. Chapter 2 will be of particular relevance to readers who have less first-hand experience of working in schools, as it identifies some of the most typical users of reading tests in schools and LEAs. The following two chapters deal with the statistical theory underpinning standardized tests – with particular reference to the implications for interpretation. The problem of interpretation is taken further in Chapter 5 which deals with the scales used by standardized tests to express a reader's ability. In Chapter 6 the ways in which tests can be used by schools is discussed.

Chapters 7 and 8 deal respectively with diagnostic and criterion-referenced reading tests – the two major alternatives to standard-ized testing. Diagnostic testing is a term used to cover a variety of materials and methods, including a number of clinical and structured techniques. Readers of Chapter 8 familiar with *Reading Tests in the Classroom* (Vincent and Cresswell, 1976), 'pre-decessor' to this book, will be disappointed to find there has been so little advance in criterion-referenced testing of reading since the mid-70's.

The remaining chapters cover a miscellaneous set of central and current topics in reading assessment. The problem of assessing non-cognitive aspects of reading is included in the issues discussed in Chapter 9 and this theme recurs in the remarks on the Assessment of Performance Unit (APU) in the chapter which follows. Chapter 11 contains some brief but essential notes on the miscellaneous themes of parents, computerized testing and the role of educational publishers, and the final chapter presents the case for more school-based initiatives in developing new tests. Finally, readers might like to consider for themselves what might have been said in a further, unwritten, chapter which would have been called 'Misuses, Abuses and Misinterpretation of Reading Tests' . . . On balance, such a chapter remains better unwritten although some hints as to its likely content can be found in extant chapters and in *Testing Children* (Gipps *et al.*, 1983). The testing of reading already has sufficient critics and this book will be concerned primarily with discussing possibilities for better practice.

CHAPTER 1

The Teaching and Testing of Reading

In most teaching, be it of reading or any other skill or subject, the teacher continuously makes judgements and forms impressions of how the learner is progressing. This can be a minute by minute classroom process. Stierer (1983) describes this process of assessment as one of 'sense making' which is 'embedded in the fabric of meaning in the classroom'. He points out that it is a 'hidden process' which takes place inside the teacher's head and cannot be directly observed. He argues that, in fact, there is a close analogy between the process of silent reading and that of the teacher's reading assessment: the teacher 'reads' the reader, taking account not only of the language produced by the reader (the 'text') but also of his or her knowledge of the reader and the setting in which the reader functions – the context. Nevertheless, there are situations in which a more public and formal account is required. This activity will be different in kind from that of informal, intuitive classroom assessment, but its general purpose – pupil appraisal – is the same. It is part of teaching skill to be able to reach fairly full and accurate judgements about pupils in a formal mode as much as in the informal one. Both parents and colleagues will actually require professional judgements of this sort from time to time. Inclusion of test results in this process is not essential but it may well prove useful.

Many teachers will feel satisfied that they know sufficient about their pupils' reading ability as a direct result of working with them in the classroom. For them, the question of a need for test results to check or validate their own judgements simply may not arise. However, there are situations in which it is at least admissible, if not essential, to supplement this with information from some other source. It may be that the teacher is simply curious to know whether a child is as 'backward for his age' as it seems. This may be idle curiosity, but it could be a reasonable desire to scrutinize or evaluate one's subjective impressions. A headteacher may wish to know whether changes in the way reading is taught in the school have led to improvements in reading standards. On a larger scale, a Local Education Authority may be concerned to identify all children in its schools who may need extra help with reading. These are examples of some of the many situations where it would be impracticable or inappropriate to rely solely upon the teacher's judgements of how well a child can read. In the first example, the teacher would need some independent yardstick of normal performance. In the second, the headteacher would be wise to include evidence that was independent of the feelings or impressions (however valid) of those involved in the innovation. In the third example, the LEA might fear that some teachers are more inclined than others to refer children for help with reading; also, such judgements can hardly avoid being relative to the particular school's general standard. In such settings – to be discussed more fully in Chapter 6 – the need is for a screening assessment which is *objective,* that is to say, one which is independent of the particular person carrying it out. It is also often essential that the assessment is *normative* or *norm-referenced.* This concept will be developed in Chapter 3. Briefly, it refers to assessment which allows an individual's reading performance to be related to the 'average'. It is also necessary for the assessment to be *reliable* and *valid.* This means that we can be reasonably confident a result places a reader accurately in relation to the average and that the assessment reflects reading rather than some other ability. It is these characteristics which constructors of *standardized* reading tests seek to achieve in the 'instruments' (i.e. tests) which they produce. Again, these will be discussed more fully in subsequent chapters.

Standardized tests express reading ability in quantitative terms. Some kind of numerical score is used to summarize a child's or group's performance. This is precise, but tells the teacher nothing in operational or qualitative terms about a child's reading. Yet it is information which does this which is of greatest importance in planning teaching or remediation. A variety of *diagnostic* reading tests which are more or less distinct from the standardized instruments is available for this purpose. It has already been observed that experienced teachers who know the children they are teaching are likely to be well-informed about their pupils' reading. Nevertheless, diagnostic tests may usefully supplement or guide such knowledge. Also, it cannot be assumed that all teachers fit into the above category, in which case some form of diagnostic test can be of great value.

It is with these two forms of reading assessment – standardized and diagnostic – that the central chapters of this book deal. The sections which follow in this chapter prepare for these by reviewing some of the background, principles and issues associated with the testing of reading.

How Reading is Tested – Types of Reading Tests

There are numerous ways in which teachers assess (as opposed to test) reading, such as hearing a child read a current reading book, recording progress through a reading scheme, monitoring the extent of borrowing from class or school libraries or conducting reading interviews with pupils. This book is concerned mainly – although not exclusively – with a sub-category of assessment, that of testing. Testing in reading is certainly a sufficiently full and specialized topic to merit a book on its own. Above all it is a relatively *technical* topic (compared to other modes of assessment), where it is practice and experience, rather than technical knowledge, which are needed. At the same time, too rigid a distinction between testing and other forms of assessment would be counter-productive. The challenge this book offers to the teacher is that of considering how better use might be made of testing as part of his or her general professional skill in assessment.

Reading tests are distinct from other means of assessment in that they are formal and prepared devices for getting information about a child's reading. Ideally, a reading test seeks to elicit the normal act of reading, or a process essential to reading, in a way which allows precise observations and judgements to be made. (How far such ideals are attained is a matter which critics of testing continue to dispute and is certainly one of which test users cannot afford to lose sight.)

The ways in which particular tests put the above ideal into practice are diverse. It is thus rather difficult to give a brief definition of what a reading test is. The best way for someone who has never seen any reading tests to get an idea of what they are would be to examine a few. It would become apparent that most consist of a printed booklet or sheet containing either material to be read aloud or questions ('items') to be answered silently. A separate handbook or manual will be provided which gives instructions for administering, marking and interpreting the test.

Pumfrey (1977, Ch. 4) has suggested a three-dimensional system for classifying reading tests according to instructional goals, sources of information (method of testing) and purposes to which information obtained will be put. The more advanced student of reading assessment will find this helpful. A somewhat simpler 'map' is presented following:

The act of reading itself can be either *oral* or *silent* and reading tests can be correspondingly divided into oral and silent. They may be further categorized by the *level of language* they test: word; sentence; continuous prose. This leads to a simple grid into which all standardized tests and many diagnostic tests can be classified:

	ORAL	SILENT
WORD		
SENTENCE		
PASSAGE		

For example, the Schonell *Graded Word Reading Test,* and *Salford Sentence Reading Test* and the *Neale Analysis of Reading Ability* involve, respectively, the oral reading of a series of words, sentences and prose passages of increasing difficulty. They thus fit into successive rows in the left hand column. Similarly, Test 1 of Brimer and Raban's *Infant Reading Test,* Level 2 of *The Primary Reading Test* and the *London Reading Test* fit into corresponding rows in the silent column. These tests all involve silent working and selection or supply of answers in printed/written form.

Oral Testing

Much testing which takes place in school involves oral tests, particularly at word and sentence level. Once purchased such tests remain available for use indefinitely as they consist of a reusable card or sheet on which lists of successively harder words or sentences are printed. The test words and sentences are themselves unrelated – thus making the reading activity largely meaningless to the child. This may be justified for certain diagnostic purposes but is otherwise indefensible. Meek (1982) has argued that 'The way children are taught to read tells them what adults think literacy is' (page 18). Meek is referring particularly to the *teaching* of reading in the initial stages. Yet surely this is a comment which applies with even greater force to the way we *assess* reading.

The use of such word and sentence reading tests is defended on the grounds that they are economical, can be administered quickly and scores can be rapidly translated into reading 'ages'. The latter concept is one which is examined critically in Chapter 5. The supposed economic advantages lead in turn to abuses, particularly over-frequent testing, with the result that some children soon know the contents of tests such as Schonell and Holborn by heart! Tests which use continuous prose for oral reading are closer to 'real' reading but there are fewer of them and they are less widely used by class teachers.

There is a further general limitation to oral testing which should be considered. As reading develops it becomes decreasingly a public and oral performance and more a personal and private activity. Reading specialists argue that teachers should encourage this and avoid fixation on reading aloud in the Middle Junior years. In turn this brings into question the relevance of testing reading orally. Standardized oral tests may well give reading ages for some years beyond 10 and 11, but this cannot be taken to imply the appropriateness of the tests for reading at this age level.

Two further limitations must be noted. Firstly, oral tests, particularly at word and sentence level, rarely take account of understanding. This makes them unsuitable for children for whom English is a second language. More generally, few reading theorists or practitioners would wish to argue that reading for meaning is not greatly more important than formal oral accuracy. Secondly, it cannot be assumed that oral reading tests are entirely objective in the sense mentioned earlier. The dividing line between a 'misreading' and a halting but accurate 'decoding' is a fine one and a teacher may be obliged to use subjective or intuitive judgement. There are also practical difficulties in counting the errors made by a reader stumbling through a difficult chunk of continuous prose.

Silent Testing

The use of silent testing avoids most of the preceding difficulties. It is possible to concentrate upon reading for meaning, not decoding. Also, silent testing lends itself to objective methods, particularly *multiple choice* items. These are test items where a fixed choice of possible answers – usually four or five – is presented and the pupil must select the correct one. This means that marking is entirely mechanical and each reader's result is in no way dependent upon the judgement of whoever is marking the test. Marking can be, and sometimes is, carried out by a machine such as an optical scanner. It must be added that 'objectivity' is sometimes undermined by clerical error or gross misunderstanding of the marking and scoring procedures.

It is also the case that most word level silent tests are really concerned with sound-symbol matching (e.g. *Carver's Word Recognition Test; Raban's Infant Reading Tests 1* and *2*) but this limitation is not intrinsic. By using a word-picture matching format, as in the early parts of the *Primary Reading Test,* it is possible to test recognition of meaning.

The scope of silent testing is greatly increased at the sentence level. Characteristically, such tests involve sentence completion (e.g. 'The bird was in its . . . . . . wing/*nest*/feather/sky') or selection of a picture which matches the meaning of a sentence. Davies (1977) and Vincent and Cresswell (1976) argue that sentence-completion items involve a use of a number of key reading skills such as knowledge of syntactical constraints, vocabulary, use of context and reading experience. Such tests also make it possible to cover a wide range of reading ability by preparing items of steeply graded difficulty. This makes them particularly useful in large-scale LEA testing and screening programmes. Nevertheless, real life reading matter rarely consists of lists of unrelated sentences and the most difficult items tend to be wordy and contrived in style. Their use is also restricted to standardized rather than diagnostic testing.

To the above reservations it could be added that intelligent reading involves use of context beyond the limit of the sentence. Chapman (1983) also discusses how learning to read requires understanding of the structural or 'cohesive' ties which make continuous prose into a meaningful running text rather than a random set of unrelated sentences or propositions.

Tests based on continuous material are more likely to include such processes in addition to those tested at word and sentence level. Silent reading of continuous prose, in particular, would also be recognized by many readers as a fairly typical activity. Here silent tests based on continuous prose material clearly have an advantage over other forms.

Silent prose reading tests are of two main types. The traditional format is for a test to contain one or more prose passages with a set of questions, usually in multiple-choice form. Test R, Reading Comprehension, of the *Richmond Test of Basic Skills* and parts of the *Edinburgh Reading Tests* series are typical examples. Continuous prose comprehension allows scope for testing a range of processes or activities, including inferential and evaluative skills. The Edinburgh series actually gives separate scores for a number of 'subtests' dealing with allegedly different reading comprehension skills. For example, the Stage 2 test, for the Middle Junior age range, covers Vocabulary, Comprehension of Sequences, Retention of Significant Details, Use of Context and Reading Rate. This elaboration has attractions, but, as later chapters will note in more detail, it is often of dubious validity.

The prose comprehension tests currently available in published form are all rather episodic. They base their questions on sets of discrete and unrelated prose passages. This is convenient for securing a gradient of reading difficulty, but hardly typifies 'real' reading. Even quite young readers will be more used to books and material which sustain a theme, narrative or topic over a number of pages, if not in a complete book. The tests currently employed by the Assessment of Performance Unit (APU) to assess national reading standards (see Chapter 10) are interesting examples of how future published tests might overcome this limitation.

CLOZE PROCEDURE

A more recent development in continuous prose comprehension testing is the 'cloze' test. A cloze test consists of a prose passage from which certain words have been deleted and replaced by underlined gaps of uniform length. The reader's task is to write in these missing words, or acceptable close synonyms:

> This is an _____ of a cloze test. You will note that a _____ of words are _____ and a blank line _____ been inserted in the _____ where the word should be.

Cloze procedure originated as a means of assessing readability of written material. Researchers have demonstrated that – as might be expected – there is a relationship between how well people can fill in missing words and other criteria of how well they understand the text (e.g. Bormuth 1968). It is not surprising to find that a technique which does this in effect measures the reading ability of those involved – better readers will find texts easier than poor readers. The technique has thus been developed for standardized testing and a range of published standardized tests based partly or entirely on cloze procedure is now available in the UK. Of these the *Bowman Test of Reading Competence* and the *London Reading Test* are probably the best examples.

Certain general conventions have been developed for the preparation of cloze passages. The extent to which these are observed varies greatly, according to the purpose for which cloze procedure is to be used. It might be said that the only definitive and invariable feature of cloze procedure is that it involves filling in gaps in a piece of language. However, it is usual for at least some of the following features to be found:

a. The test is in written rather than oral form.
b. It consists of more than one sentence.
c. Gaps are marked by blank lines of uniform length.
d. Missing words have to be written in by the reader rather than be chosen from a multiple choice set. (This latter multiple choice variation has been termed 'maze' procedure.)
e. The first sentence is complete to allow a lead in.

f. Words are deleted at a rate of frequency equivalent to no more than one word in five.

g. Adjacent words are not deleted, allowing some 'bilateral' context.

These conventions are usually applied in constructing cloze-based reading tests. However, testing raises three further special considerations – criteria for deleting words, length of test passage and marking criteria.

In some applications of cloze, words are deleted randomly. Over a sustained passage this will provide the fairest indication of the difficulty of the text. For preparing passages for standardized tests it is customary to delete words selectively to ensure the test presents a range of difficulty, avoiding words which would be near impossible to guess or words which are so easy (in technical terms, so 'redundant') that very few readers are unable to supply them. In many experimental uses of cloze procedure it has been judged necessary to use passages of at least 300 words in length. This would allow distinctive qualities of style or thought to be revealed and provide a far-reaching context which might be tested by particular deleted words. In fact, while published cloze test passages vary in length, according to the whim of the test author, few use passages of this length. It is more common to use a succession of unrelated passages, perhaps of graded readability. Many of these are probably too short to allow for the use of far-reaching contextual clues.

In the purest form of cloze procedure only the originally deleted word counts as a correct response. Researchers have shown that for measuring readability of texts or estimating reading ability, little improvement in validity is secured by allowing 'equally good' synonyms. The practice of insisting that all answers except the original deleted word must be marked wrong – however valid and convenient – would raise considerable problems in any published test for routine use in school. In practice published examples do allow limited numbers of alternative responses. The test constructors may also mitigate the problem by favouring items which do not lend themselves to many alternatives.

Cloze tests tend to agree closely with other conventional tests of reading ability. It is certainly possible to speculate that cloze tasks involve a range of processes which are central to reading comprehension. For example, Rye (1982) suggests that cloze involves word recognition, use of semantic, syntactic and stylistic features of text to infer or predict, and skills of skimming and scanning. Chapman (1983, Chapter 8) suggests it can be used to test the development of knowledge of *cohesion* – the principles by which sentences in a continuous text are related to or tie up with one another.

Rye also gives the fullest discussion so far published of practical use of cloze as a teaching technique. Discussion of its teaching applications are also found in Walker (1974) and Lunzer and Gardner (1979). It must be said in passing that the technique may become yet another form of unproductive busy work in some schools (children fill gaps; teachers fill time). It is perhaps best used as a basis for group exercises rather than an easy way of creating classwork.

Although few published cloze tests are concerned with correct spelling it seems that cloze could involve a heavier writing load than other forms of reading test. Also, there are few 'real life' reading tasks which require the filling in of missing words. Yet in other respects cloze tests would seem to involve similar reading skills to those covered by conventional tests requiring use of context and inference.

Reading Rate

It would have been possible to add a third dimension to the two sets of categories by which reading tests have been classified by including rate or speed of reading. In at least some categories there can be found tests which are timed or include a measure based on time taken, as opposed to 'untimed' tests, which have no time factor. For example, the *Neale Analysis of Reading Ability* incorporates a separate measure for rate of reading, while the NFER *EH3* test is completed against the clock. It is less easy to suggest examples of speeded, paced or timed test at the word and sentence level. However, in the 'Black Museum of Reading Tests' can be found the *Ballard One-Minute Reading Test* which consists of a list of unrelated words of which as many as possible must be read aloud in sixty seconds! In practice, speeded or timed reading tests have not proved popular with British teachers and even those still in print are not widely used. Most popular reading tests are untimed and are designed on the assumption that all children will have time to tackle all the items or tasks in a test. Technically this is referred to as 'power' testing. At the same time, the administration instructions for many tests include a specific time limit. Sometimes, such timing is imposed in what is really a power test as an administrative convenience designed to minimize the amount of time needed to give the test and ensure weaker readers are not exposed too long to a difficult task. It is assumed that in the time limit allowed a reader will have tackled all the items she or he would be capable of answering correctly. This is often the practice with silent sentence-completion tests which present items in steeply graded order of difficulty.

Paced or timed measures of reading are often found to be unrelated to other criteria, such as accuracy or comprehension. The extent of their importance is not clear and many teachers would feel that flexibility – capacity to adjust rate of reading to the requirements of the task in hand – is of much greater importance than sheer speed for its own sake.

Adequacy of Reading Tests

One way of evaluating a reading test would be to judge the extent to which it matched the prospective user's conception of what reading is. There are various alternative models of reading which reflect the different stances and perspectives of those who adopt them. Many of these do not lend themselves to a corresponding test or set of tests. Moreover, as Goodacre (1979) has pointed out, some of the main traditional preoccupations of reading test constructors differ from those of either the reading teacher or reading researcher. In effect, test constructors have often developed their tests without great reflection on the nature of what they were setting out to test.

The main criticism which arises from this neglect is that tests deal only with elementary or mechanical features of reading. For example, Stibbs (1979) suggests that reading ability includes the following hierarchy of elements:

1. Knowing the print conventions of language.
2. Associating printed symbols with sound.

3. Recognizing concepts or experiences denoted by separate words.
4. Comprehending the meanings of words in immediate contexts.
5. Making meaning in a wider context.
6. Responding personally to a text.

He argues that no existing standardized tests take account of elements 5 or 6. Later he takes reading comprehension tests to task for failing to assess use of context, appreciation of overall structure, shape and development of a passage and real life *purposes* for reading.

Stibbs' critique exemplifies particularly clearly the concerns and misgivings which many thoughtful teachers hold about reading assessment, and, indeed, language testing generally. Some of the criticisms may not be entirely justified. For example, many tests at the continuous prose level do entail use of context. Others may be met through the future production of more enlightened tests which take a wider-ranging approach to reading. The actual hierarchical analysis offered by Stibbs is, also, only one of many possible accounts of reading.

However, none of this entirely dissolves the central problems which accounts such as Stibbs' exemplify:

1. Most reading tests deal only with particular features of reading which – especially at the word level – it may be dangerous to test in isolation.

2. The majority of reading tests concentrate upon low-level, elementary or mechanical features of reading.

3. Some of the most important and valued aspects of reading remain untested, either because they are untestable or because test constructors have so far failed to consider them.

It is essential to be aware of these in selecting or using a reading test. There will be situations in which they constitute good grounds for not using a standardized test at all. Finally, they emphasize the point – well appreciated by most teachers who do use tests – that they cannot be used in isolation to appraise or make decisions about children.

Reading Assessment as Measurement

Finally, something should be said about the 'measurability' of reading ability. It is not always appreciated that much of the standard 'technology' behind reading tests – particularly standardized ones – comes directly from the more general field of psychological and mental measurement. Some inkling of this can be gained by considering the names of early British reading test authors. Most of these (e.g. Burt, Vernon, Schonell, Watts) were primarily psychologists with a major interest in intelligence and educational backwardness. Of these only Schonell appears to have taken an especial interest in reading. Their model for the assessment of reading was thus that model which already existed for the assessment of general intelligence. Some of its key principles – particularly that of the 'norm' – have already been mentioned, and Chapter 3 deals with these in further detail. Here it would be worth noting one fundamental point. This is the assumption that reading is in some sense a *measurable* entity. This entity is spoken of as 'ability', 'attainment' or 'achievement' – the terms are really interchangeable as far as reading is concerned. To be measurable reading would have to be a fixed determinable property which each reader 'has' in varying amounts. An associated assumption is that no instrument can measure reading ability with one hundred per cent accuracy. Thus any 'observed' or 'obtained' score will imperfectly reflect a reader's 'true' ability. A test score, strictly speaking, is no more than an estimate of this assumed true ability.

There is a body of research which tends to support the 'measurable reading ability' hypothesis. The majority of relevant studies have found close relationships between seemingly different tests of reading ability. This has been taken as evidence that they all tap some general underlying ability and should be borne in mind when considering the apparent differences in the six categories of reading tests discussed above.

It is also a simple matter to show that given the same test twice, or two equivalent tests, many children will *not* get exactly the same score on each occasion. Constructors of reading tests are also usually at great pains to verify the extent of such discrepancies. As a result of these they will give precise statistical estimates of the degree of error associated with their tests.

Such principles also seem to accord with the everyday wisdom of the classroom: teachers readily speak of 'good', 'poor' and 'average' readers in a way which suggests these distinctions can be relied upon and have some general currency. There are, also, many teachers who prefer to treat test results as circumstantial evidence, rather than immutable truths, although as the ETSP has shown (Gipps *et al.*, Chapter 8) this treatment can be somewhat partial. Unexpectedly favourable results may be given more credence than unfavourable ones by some teachers while others are more inclined to confine their credence to unexpectedly pessimistic ones.

While the concept of measurable ability or achievement has provided a useful basis whereby teachers can appraise their pupils it is not without limitations. There are alternative ways of approaching reading assessment which do not require the assumption of an underlying ability. One way is to think of reading in terms of tasks or skills a reader can or cannot perform. Chapter 8, Criterion Referenced Testing, deals with an important example, There are also dangers in confusing reading ability with reading potential. A child with a low reading ability test score is not necessarily destined to remain a poor reader. Even if reading ability is a determinable entity it is not an all-determining one.

Finally, no balanced view of reading teaching would focus exclusively on the aim of increasing reading 'ability'. Attitudes, values, interests and habits are also part of reading development. These are more difficult to test and as a result there is a danger they will become devalued in comparison to sheer achievement.

CHAPTER 2

Who Uses Reading Tests?

It is essential that anyone using standardized reading tests has a clear idea of what purposes they can be used for. These are reviewed in Chapter 6, after some of the main technical features of standardized tests have been outlined. Before exploring these more technical issues it would be useful to anticipate the discussion of purposes for testing by consideration of who uses – or gives – such tests. This will introduce issues of use and purpose in a way which may add relevance to the technical matter in the following chapters.

The above distinction between using and giving or administering a test is important. It has been claimed that tests have a part to play in the teaching of reading. Yet it would be simplistic to assume that they are therefore only useful to people actively involved in teaching. Most reading tests are certainly administered to pupils by their teachers, but this has often been commissioned by someone else. At times the teacher will seem to be no more than the grudging agent of a higher administrative power. It is thus worth considering briefly the varying perspectives of those involved.

Educational Psychologists

Two kinds of people actually administer reading tests to children: educational psychologists and teachers. Educational psychologists undergo specific training which qualifies them to use a range of specialized psychological tests. By contrast it is assumed that most reading tests – particularly objective group tests – could be administered and scored by any normally intelligent and responsible adult without training. Reading tests, although used by educational psychologists, are not as specialized as some of the other tests used by these professionals. There is thus no official professional demarcation between the reading tests used by psychologists and these used by teachers. In practice psychologists have customarily used individual tests such as *The Neale Analysis of Reading Ability* and parts of Daniels and Diack's *Standard Reading Tests* because their work involves assessment of individual children. Information from these tests will be used alongside results of other psychological tests in making an assessment of a child. This work is not restricted to assessment of children with reading problems. Educational psychologists occasionally also need to assess reading ability of average and exceptionally able readers. In-depth testing of individual children who have been referred for specialized appraisal has been a traditional role of the educational psychologist.

Nevertheless, it would be misleading to represent the contemporary educational psychologist as no more than a high-powered test specialist. Psychologists take on a variety of roles within an education service. Not all educational psychologists are primarily concerned with testing or with reading. Also, there has probably been a general lessening in the extent to which educational psychologists generally use tests in their work.

At the same time, psychologists continue to be concerned with the testing of reading in a number of other important, but indirect, ways. In many LEAs they are responsible for the planning and direction of authority-wide screeening and monitoring exercises. This may even include the construction of tests specifically designed for local needs. They will also advise generally on the selection and use of tests in schools.

Specialist Teachers

Remedial and reading advisory teachers, whether members of a central team or based in particular schools, are also often concerned with assessment of individual readers. In recent years such teachers have probably taken on some of the responsibilities for reading difficulty which were previously the remit of educational psychologists. Like psychologists, they may use both standardized and diagnostic tests to appraise children who have been referred by teachers who suspect they may need remedial help. Unlike psychologists they will be more specifically concerned with testing literacy rather than other mental processes and will probably place greater additional emphasis upon tests which provide immediate guidance for their own teaching. They may also use standardized tests to monitor the progress of their pupils. Reading test results may also impinge upon the work of advisory teachers in that results of LEA-wide surveys (see below and Chapter 6) may determine to which schools they are allocated.

It has been pointed out that psychologists vary in the extent to which they rely upon reading tests in their work. This applies with even greater emphasis to specialist reading and remedial teachers. Some teachers working in this area have deep-seated objections to testing – perhaps because their work too often brings them into contact with schools where tests are misused or misinterpreted. Thus, it would be misleading to represent them as a group in favour of testing, although the group certainly includes teachers who do find reading tests particularly valuable for some of their work.

Primary School Class Teachers

Many of the assessment requirements of Primary school class teachers are not dissimilar from those of the reading or remedial specialist. The most marked difference is that class teachers will be concerned with assessment and recording of progress in a much larger number of children. This might seem to imply a greater need for group testing although in practice class teachers seem to make greatest use of poor quality, out of date individual tests such as Schonell, Burt and Holborn – probably because such reusable tests are most likely to be to hand. It may also be that there is a ritual need for oral testing in line with the traditional method of teaching children to read by hearing them read. Class teachers are also often required to administer tests at the behest of others, particularly the headteacher or the LEA. They will also probably be required to mark and record results but do not necessarily always see themselves as active partners in such assessment exercises.

Primary Headteachers

Headteachers of Primary schools have a crucial role in the testing of reading. It is they who will be responsible for any school-wide policy of regular testing and they will be influential in determining which tests are used and what they are used for. The ETSP found that 75 per cent of the schools in their sample employed some form of reading test. This reflects widespread confidence in the value of testing at this senior professional level.

Heads have a particular concern with maintenance of standards and progress, as well as identification of children in need of additional help. One way of meeting all of these requirements is by testing all children in a target age or year group. This is most often done by class teachers using group or individual tests on the instruction of a headteacher. However, some heads prefer to do this personally, even if it involves individual testing of all the children concerned. While this ensures consistency, it may seem to make unwarranted demands upon time. However, one of the most serious concerns to arise from ETSP was the strong possibility that teachers vary greatly in the actual way they will administer and mark the same test. Substantial departures from specified procedures over timing, instructions, permitted assistance and criteria for correct responses can invalidate test results. Yet the ETSP findings suggest that such departures may not be uncommon and that the results will later be used by others who are unaware of them. Where a headteacher takes personal responsibility for testing there is likely to be much more consistency. Many heads may well choose to do all the testing with the explicit intention of ensuring the standard administration procedures are observed. Such an undertaking has the additional incidental advantage of providing a basis for personal contact with children not necessarily taught by the headteacher. This is one of several interesting instances where testing seems to fulfil a useful role, but, on reflection, it appears that a standardized reading test is by no means indispensable for the purpose in hand.

Senior staff can have a similar influence on testing in secondary schools. The majority of standardized testing is carried out in the first year of secondary school and the decision to test may well rest with a deputy/year head rather than the headteacher. With the exception of diagnostic testing carried out by remedial teachers in the way already described, most testing of reading is for managerial purposes similar to those which concern Primary heads. The difference is that this is much more likely to involve silent group tests and it is rare for senior teachers to administer individual tests personally.

Local Education Authorities

Finally, the influence of LEA advisers and administrators should be mentioned. These officials share – on an authority-wide scale – the managerial interests of Primary and Secondary heads in screening, standards and progress. They may also need to know about variations between schools and areas or wish to use test results as a guide to resource allocation. These concerns have led to the use of group attainment tests on a large scale in many authorities, as a recent survey by Gipps and Wood (1981) showed. Such testing is sometimes termed 'blanket' testing because it is designed to include all children in the selected age groups. Often, it will involve testing and re-testing children two or three times in their school careers

The ETSP report discusses in considerable detail the use of standardized tests by LEAs. They note that 'political', 'managerial' or 'professional' motives may have caused the introduction of testing by LEAs. Of these, the lattermost, exemplified by screening and transfer testing to pass on relevant information about individual pupils to new schools, are the least contentious. They are also likely to be the most enduring. However, the ETSP researchers found some confusion over the purposes of LEA testing. In particular, they felt that some LEAs were unrealistic in expecting one test to fill a multiplicity of roles. There were also instances where large numbers of test results had been obtained but thereafter were not acted upon in any way.

It will have become evident that all too often class teachers find themselves giving tests for purposes formulated by others. In fact it is highly likely they will have access to the results of the tests they have been asked to give. The ETSP found that results of LEA tests were widely used by the schools themselves for record keeping, screening, checking progress and providing 'feedback on teaching' – topics to be enlarged upon in Chapter 6. Unfortunately this more or less 'voluntary' interest in test results may be misplaced. The ETSP researchers express concern about the 'disjunction' between the purpose of LEA testing and the actual purpose to which test results are put by the schools who carry out testing. Headteachers, class teachers and the instigators of an LEA testing programme all appear to have different perceptions of its purpose. Even where the same word is used to describe purpose of testing its meaning may vary. For example, 'grouping' on the basis of test results may be a synonym for 'streaming' amongst headteachers while it may refer to a much more transient form of setting when employed by class teachers. The ETSP findings also suggest there may be instances where teachers make entirely inappropriate use of results. Certainly, it does not follow that a test chosen for large-scale LEA surveys will be directly relevant to teaching. This is partly due to the purpose of testing which necessitates a particular type of test.

Furthermore, to act judiciously on test results one needs to be able to interpret them. Expertise of this sort has not been regarded as a conventional part of the teacher's professional training. Nevertheless, there is a strong case for now treating technical expertise in assessment in this way. Indeed, the ETSP report calls for creation of posts of special responsibility for assessment in schools. Even though there may be dangers in divorcing assessment of reading from its teaching by establishing assessment 'generalists', the proposal is one which deserves serious consideration.

CHAPTER 3

Principles of Standardized Testing

The great majority of published reading tests are *standardized*. The practical implication of this is that a child's raw score (the total number of correct responses) can be equated with some kind of standard, usually the average for the relevant age group. The process of establishing a set of standards involves the testing of fairly large groups of children who are representative of age groups for which the test is intended. Only then is a test said to be standardized, and, for better or worse, only then will many teachers want to buy and use it. Whatever other virtues a test may have, the availability of tables to convert raw scores to some kind of scaled score, such as a reading 'Age' or 'Quotient' seems a precondition for commercial success. This has meant that only certain people have been in a position to construct standardized reading tests. It is mainly research agencies such as the National Foundation for Educational Research (NFER), LEA educational psychologists or researchers in institutions of Higher Education who will have the resources, expertise and access to large samples of children necessary for developing standardized tests.

Normative Testing

The term 'normative' or 'norm-referenced' is often used as a synonym for 'standardized'. This reflects one of the main uses and assumptions surrounding standardized tests. The average, standard or norm is adopted as a yardstick against which to compare individual children or groups. There are often sound reasons for wishing to compare a child with the 'norm'. Some of these uses are reviewed in Chapter 6. However, there are myriads of pitfalls associated with the concept of a 'norm'. In particular, it is easy to confuse the 'norm' with the 'ideal', or to adopt an unquestioned medical analogy; 'below average reading ability' is *not* the same as 'below normal blood pressure'! In fact, standardized tests are designed specifically to spread out or discriminate between readers of different ability. In a 'normal' group of children there will be those who are below average – the norm – and those who are above. The headteacher (sadly not apocryphal) who bemoaned the fact that 'nearly half the children admitted to the school were below average' was simply betraying ignorance of standardized testing. In a truly 'normal' group of children half *would* be below the average. This should make it clear that standardized testing has a technical side. To use standardized tests some knowledge of their technicalities is mandatory. How does one go about acquiring this knowledge?

Statistical Background and Principles of Test Construction

These technicalities are mainly statistical and have relatively little to do with reading as such. There are numerous British and American textbooks on educational measurement and statistics in general which cover the relevant principles. Most college and university education department libraries will have at least two or three suitable examples – this is a field in which there has been a steady flow of publications. A number of works also tackle the subject with special reference to reading assessment. These might be regarded as 'second level' reading upon completion of this book. Further notes of guidance on both general and reading-specific texts are given at the end of this chapter. Finally, it should not be overlooked that the manuals themselves of some standardized tests give clear accounts of the technical bases of the tests they accompany. The Manual for Spooncer's *Group Literacy Assessment*, for example, gives a helpful guidance on the interpretation of the normative scoring system used.

Standardized Testing: Technical Features

For readers who do not happen to have immediate access to these sources the following sections briefly review the main technical features of standardized testing. To do this it is necessary to refer to some of the key procedures which have to be carried out with pilot or prototype versions of a test prior to its publication. It might seem to the uninitiated that it is the particular skill which went into the writing or devising of the test items, i.e. questions, which must set the standardized test apart from anything that could be devised in the classroom. There is some truth in the claim that writing educational test items is a definite skill. However, it is in the technical activities required for selecting and validating items and in the establishment of norms that the greatest differences are to be found.

Item Analysis

Before a test can be standardized a number of item vetting exercises must be carried out. This process is referred to as item analysis. It commences by preparing trial versions of the test which contain, overall, more items than will probably be needed in the final version. The trial tests are administered to groups of approximately 300 children of the age and ability range for which the test is intended. The aim is to weed out items which do not aid the overall test in spreading out the scores. Items which everyone can do, or nobody can do, would clearly make no contribution. The percentage of pupils passing an item is termed its *facility index*, and in practice, items with facilities of less than 30 per cent or more than 70 per cent are discarded or used sparingly. For maximum spread an overall or average facility of 50 per cent in the set of items is desirable. Also, a *discrimination index* is obtained for each item. This is a measure of the item's capacity to distinguish between readers of greater and lesser ability. A number of methods are available for doing this. All reflect the principle that ideally an item should not be *passed* by readers of *lower ability than, or equal ability to,* ones who *fail* it. More simply, good readers should give correct responses to the items and poor readers should give incorrect responses. 'Good readers' are usually defined as those who score highly on the whole test and 'poor readers' those who score poorly. Perfect discrimination, expressed as +1.0, is rare but test constructors will look for items which come as close to this as possible. Test constructors tend not to report the facility or discrimination values of items in the finally published version of a test and the user has to take it on trust that the selection has been judicious.

These two criteria, particularly that of a range of item difficulty, may be at odds with those which teachers apply in much of their day to day work with children:

THE SCENE: A school staffroom. The 'Test Constructor' is visiting the school to find out what the staff think of a new reading test which is undergoing trials in the school. Horrified Teacher of 2C has just finished looking through their results:

Horrified Teacher: This new reading test is *dreadful*! Some of my weaker readers can only do the first five or six questions!
Test Constructor: That's because they're not as good at reading as the rest of the class . . .
Horrified Teacher: . . . and one or two quite good readers found the last five or six very hard!
Test Constructor: It seems I got at least a few of the items in the right order.
Horrified Teacher: . . . and look at this question: *half the class* couldn't do it! And we *know* they're really quite average children!
Test Constructor: Well, we found that item did have a facility index of fifty per cent when we tried it out before.
Horrified Teacher: But there are *lots more* questions like that!
Test Constructor: There have to be if the test is to measure effectively across the ability range.
Horrified Teacher: Yes, but only the top fifty per cent of my class could do most of these questions.
Test Constructor: Sounds as if they could have quite a high discrimination index.
Horrified Teacher: Do you mean to say your test deliberately discriminates against poor readers?
Test Constructor: Yes, otherwise it wouldn't be any use. We discard items which don't discriminate.

Horrified Teacher: But I spend most of my time trying to find reading activities which my children *can* do! I certainly don't want to discriminate against the weaker ones by giving them stuff they can't read.

Test Constructor: Er, perhaps that's part of the difference between testing and teaching – *(Fortunately, the bell is heard for the next lesson.)*

These two methods of item-analysis are occasionally supplemented by more sophisticated forms of statistical treatment. One of the more controversial of these is Rasch analysis. This involves estimation of an absolute item 'difficulty' index which is assumed to be independent of the abilities of the children who happened to be involved in the trials. An initial idea of the technique can be gained from considering the rank ordering of questions in relative difficulty to one another: if able readers find question A harder than question B one would expect that relationship to be consistent when the items are attempted by another group of less able readers. It would be reasonable to reject items with rankings that were found to vary according to the ability of the readers upon whom they were tried. Rasch analysis employs a special estimate of item difficulty rather than simple ranking, but the principle is the same. If trials with groups of different ability result in significantly different difficulty values for certain items these would be candidates for exclusion from the final test. This method is discussed further in the next chapter.

Standardization

Once unsuitable items have been discarded a final version of the test will be compiled for standardization. This requires a sample of readers who are representative of the types of readers for whom the test is intended. This sample will provide a reference point for evaluating scores of any readers who are tested in future. For commercially published tests this sample is usually chosen to be representative of the national age group. Occasionally some more 'local' group is used, such as certain age groups within an LEA or region.

In practice, these credentials of a standardized test are too often taken on trust. In the first place, there is no absolute reason for taking a national group as a reference point. In any case, there are alternative ways of defining a national sample of an age group. For example, children in special and private schools (surely part of a full national picture?) are rarely included in the standardization of reading tests. Strictly speaking, the reference group on which a standardized test is based is termed the *population*. Populations are comprehensive groups which include everyone with a specified attribute or set of attributes. These attributes are defined *arbitrarily* by the test developer to provide a reference group which is likely to seem relevant to teachers who will use the test. For example, a test standardized on a sample selected to represent a population defined as 'all children attending LEA and maintained Junior schools in September 1984' would probably be judged relevant for assessing most children in the 7 to 11 age range.

However, there would be many 7 to 11 year-olds who would not be included in the specified population – those in First and Middle schools, for example. Test norms refer only to the population for which the test was standardized. The test user has to judge whether they are applicable to particular cases. Unfortunately, there are no precise guidelines for such applicability. One cannot say for any particular child that there are certain populations against which she or he *should* be compared and others against which she or he should not. Even if it seems likely that the child has many, or all of the attributes which define the standardization population, there is still no absolute reason for saying the norms are appropriate. An apparent match between readers and standardization population may appeal to one's preference for symmetry or for comparing 'like with like'. There are also many situations in which it is informative to compare children with their peers; for example, in tempering the expectations of over-ambitious parents. Nevertheless it is worth pausing to ask *why* so much importance has been attached to normative comparisons, and, more specifically, why comparisons with national standards have been so particularly favoured.

In fact, no published reading test *has* ever been standardized on a directly representative national sample of children. Instead, the best that test constructors have been able to achieve is a group of children in a national sample of *schools* in which all the children have been tested. This is certainly an adequate approximation for practical purposes. Many tests are based on norms for the complete population of children in a single LEA, or a group of two or more LEAs. It is unlikely that any one LEA will exactly reflect the national standard. The latter is, indeed, an ephemeral concept as it is made up out of the performance of large numbers of children who reflect widely different local standards. A selected group of LEAs may give a more balanced picture and is a common procedure for reading test standardization. Nevertheless, it would be naive to assume that a 'true' national standard is provided by such tests. Test norms are, in brief, much more arbitrary and inexact than is sometimes assumed. It is therefore not surprising that different tests will give different results for the same children.

Most standardized test norms are based on results for large numbers of readers. It sometimes seems that the larger the number, the better the test. Actually, the *source* of the standardization sample is more important than its *size*. Large numbers of children in one LEA are less likely to reflect national standards than smaller numbers in a random sample of schools throughout the country. The restriction of standardization to a limited number of LEAs is usually a compromise of convenience based on the willingness of the authority to allow testing to be carried out in local schools. It is often easier to test all the children in one area (a 'local population') than it is to negotiate testing of selected children in a nationwide sample. The former local population approach may provide results for a reassuringly large number of children. It will also allow differences between age groups to be clearly delineated. Provided the 'localized' nature of the norms is understood the standardization should be adequate as a simple – if arbitrary – yardstick against which to compare children. However, standardization on a national sample would probably have a somewhat different set of norms and could be conducted adequately with no more, if not fewer children.

Evaluating a Standardized Test

It would be reasonable to ask how, merits of content and approach to reading aside, one can tell a well-standardized test from a bad one. There are two initial criteria that can be applied. Standardization should have been *recent* and should have been carried out on a *relevant* sample of readers. Evidence from past national surveys of reading suggest that standards change with time. It would be hazardous to define 'recency' exactly, but norms over 15 years old become increasingly suspect. Relevance of norms depends greatly upon the user's purpose and the interpretation placed upon results. Normal practice is to assume that norms must provide a 'national' average against which to compare children. However, more 'local' norms are sometimes available and there is no absolute criterion for saying that national rather than local norms are the 'right' ones to use. The *London Reading Test*, for example, provides separate norms for ILEA pupils. These are somewhat more lenient, reflecting slightly lower overall performance in the ILEA compared with the rest of the UK. However, in evaluating school standards and progress, an ILEA teacher might feel that local norms were more realistic.

In establishing local norms it is often possible to give the test to all the children in the age groups for which the test is designed. Where this is done the 'representativeness' of the resulting norm is not open to question. However, when the norm is intended to reflect standards in a much larger group than is actually tested, the way in which the standardization group is selected is crucial.

The procedures employed in the standardization of the four stages of the *Edinburgh Reading Tests* exemplify the way test constructors attempt to select representative samples of pupils. For each stage the constructors commenced by dividing England and Wales into ten areas. The test manuals do not identify these areas, but state they were designed to contain equal portions of the population. Two LEAs were then selected from within each area. In each case one was a county authority, the other a borough. Five or six schools were selected randomly from each authority. One class of approximately 30 children was then chosen within each school, providing a nominal sample of 3000 children overall. In practice the final samples were smaller due to non-response or withdrawal of schools. The constructors also report that classes were selected to ensure balance of sexes and even distribution across the age range for standardization. Similar procedures were carried out separately for Scotland. The resulting sample contained children from a wide cross-section of schools. Moreover, the schools were selected randomly from within a representative sample of LEAs, which would mean the resulting group of schools would be a reasonable approximation to a genuinely represent-ative national sample. However, the resulting norms could not be regarded as true national norms. As the constructors found in standardizing Stage 2, the younger children in the sample appeared to come from schools where the general standard was probably higher than average. Also, while it is evident that the tests were standardized in the early to mid 70s, exact years and times of year for this are not given. This introduces an additional need for caution in using the norms. However, to achieve appreciably greater precision in the norms would have probably required a disproportionately more complex and expensive stand-ardization exercise.

A similar technique for obtaining a representative sample was used by the constructor of the *Primary Reading Test*. In this case the ten regions are clearly identified as those used in official DES statistics and all LEAs in each region were involved. Every 70th school within each LEA was included in the sample, a procedure slightly superior to that used for the Edinburgh tests, albeit at the cost of requiring more LEAs to participate. The development of this test is also noteworthy for the use of large and representative groups of children in the early trials of prototype items.

In the construction of both tests there has been a clear intention at least to approach national representativeness. This approach is somewhat different to that found in many other tests – particularly earlier ones – where no details of the sample are given or the norms are based on results of testing a large number of children concentrated in one or two areas. It should be added that while this latter technique is by no means invalid the associated norms can be equated with 'national' norms with much less confidence.

'Most of my class wouldn't even be able to read the instructions, let alone do the questions!'

There is one further less statistical aspect of evaluating stand-ardized tests which should be referred to here. This concerns the criteria by which tests get to be selected. From Chapter 1 it will have emerged that there are great variations in content and that teachers need to consider how, if at all, the test's model of reading might be relevant to his or her purpose. In this chapter certain statistical criteria have been discussed – item analysis and standardization. It has been stressed that adequacy of standard-ization, particularly recency and relevance of norms, should also be a major consideration in appraising a test. Little is known about how, in practice, teachers select tests. Cheapness, ease of administration and scoring and established reputation are prob-ably important. However, certain types of reactions should *not* be permitted to influence a decision. The temptation should be avoided to glance casually at a few items, pick on one which seems on superficial inspection to be ambiguous ('*I* can't do that one, so how do they expect the children to be able to do it?') and condemn the test out of hand. Reading tests are written to be read in a particular way, by a particular type of reader. A child working purposefully and with concentration in class may have much less difficulty with an item than an adult who flicks through the test and picks it out at random. Secondly, the potential difficulty of the test should not be overestimated. Teachers sometimes express alarm at the apparent difficulty of new test material. Yet a test which was perfectly matched to their class would contain many items which, by design, half the children would fail. Also, there may be a tendency for some teachers to be over-protective of their pupils and either to underrate their capacity to do a particular reading task or overrate the stress it will occasion. There is no substitute for giving the tests a fair trial with a cross-section of pupils. It may be that the continued preference for archaic tests in schools is due in part to misapprehensions about the 'difficulty' of newer alternatives.

Suggestions for Further Reading

A.C. Crocker's *Statistics for the Teacher* and D. Rowntree's *Statistics Without Tears* both present clear introductions to the concepts of normal distribution and the standard deviation which underpin concepts outlined in this and the following chapters. Vincent and Cresswell (1976) and Pumfrey (1977) present accounts which refer directly to reading and cover the topics in more detail than is attempted in the present book. Certain chapters in Raggett *et al.* (1979) also deal with statistical aspects of reading assessment. There are also a number of excellent American texts on educational and psychological measurement.

Although usually lengthy, these texts are clear, well-illustrated and written at an introductory level. R.L. Thorndike and E. Hagen *Measurement and Evaluation in Psychology and Education*, A. Anastasi's *Psychological Testing* and L.J. Cronbach's *Essentials of Psychological Measurement* are typical examples which are likely to be found in many institutional libraries with an education section.

The most highly recommendable of currently available texts is Satterly's *Assessment in Schools*. This is referred to at a number of points in this book as it gives extended yet clear coverage of topics in greater depths than is appropriate in an introductory text. Satterly provides a particularly full introduction to statistical aspects of educational measurement as well as many important but less technical topics. The text should be regarded as the standard reference source on assessment for British teachers.

CHAPTER 4

Reliability and Validity

In addition to adequacy of item analysis characteristics, standardization and content, a test must possess the qualities of reliability
and validity. These are outlined in this chapter.

Reliability

The manuals for all properly constructed standardized tests
contain some evidence concerning 'reliability'. This is desirable, if
not essential, for any published test. A reliable test is one which
would give the 'same result' if given to the same readers on a
different occasion. To put it more technically, a perfectly reliable
test would always place each person tested in his or her true
position exactly, relative to the mean. In real life this does not
happen. Children's concentration and motivation certainly fluc-
tuate from day to day and chance slips of the pen or tongue and
isolated misunderstandings on the part of either reader or test
administrator will also colour test performance on any particular
occasion. A list of potential factors which could prevent children
doing their absolute best on a test would be long. For example, a
Primary school teacher might wish to consider the likely consequences of giving a test on a windy day as opposed to any other,
or after a break period when torrential rain has made it impossible
for the children to go into the playground. No test can be immune
to such gross influences. Nevertheless, it is important to establish
that a test is not intrinsically prone to variations and fluctuations
because of its actual design or content and that, external
conditions aside, it gives a dependable picture of reading ability. A
number of standard techniques are used to this end.

Test-retest Reliability

The most direct way of assessing reliability is actually to give the same test twice to a group of children and compare the two sets of results. The extent of the agreement can be expressed as a statistical index, the reliability coefficient. A coefficient of 1.0 would represent perfect agreement but in practice values of .85 and above are taken as indicating an acceptable level of reliability. The notion of giving the same test twice and expecting to get the same score from each child on each occasion may seem somewhat naive. Surely, children will do better second time round, as a result of familiarity and practice? In fact, the test constructor does not rely upon a literal matching of the two sets of raw scores. If there is an upward increase, however, it is important that it is fairly uniform so that not only do children's rank orders remain the same, but their standing in relation to the overall mean on each occasion remains approximately constant. Thus, the technique does not require that each reader obtains exactly the same score on both occasions, but that each score should remain in the same position relative to the mean of the two sets of scores. For example, if a child is asked to re-read an oral continuous prose test there is a strong possibility that some words mis-read on the first occasion will be correctly read on the second. Also, some words, read correctly the first time, may be mis-read at the second attempt. However, if this phenomenon is general to a group of children tested, so that their rank order remains the same across the two occasions, and there is no systematic tendency for some children to make disproportionately fewer – or more – errors on re-reading, then the test will display adequate test-retest reliability.

Parallel Forms Reliability

In the section on item analysis in Chapter 3 it was mentioned that test constructors sometimes tried out a pool of items so that multiple versions of a test could be produced. These alternative versions are said to be equivalent or parallel if there is a close match in content and item difficulty and each version gives the same mean and distribution of scores. Sometimes test reliability is based on the agreement between such parallel forms when administered to the same children. This is similar in principle to simple test-retest reliability but it excludes any effects of recall or specific practice on the second set of test results. Again, reliability coefficients of greater than .85 would be expected. However, in both methods the strength of the agreement will be partly affected by the length of time between the first and second testing occasions. The longer this hiatus, the more likely it will be that changes will occur, at least in certain children, which will make an exact match between the two sets of results impossible. Nevertheless, it is essential that a high degree of general agreement is maintained across the two tests.

Internal Consistency Reliability

There is a group of techniques for establishing reliability based on the statistical analysis of results from a single administration of a test. The simplest of these involves splitting the test into two halves, say odd and even-numbered items, and comparing the two sets of scores. A 'split-half' reliability coefficient is computed on the basis of this agreement. There are some more advanced techniques, which take account of the many possible ways a test could be split into two halves and thus give a more 'reliable' estimate of reliability. Kuder Richardson formulas 20 and 21 and Cronbach's Alpha are the most widely used of these for reading tests. These methods are usually referred to as 'internal consistency' reliability coefficients.

Because they are free of the real life vagaries of testing the same children twice they tend to give larger positive coefficients. More stringent criteria must thus be applied to internal consistency coefficients. Values less than .90 suggest questionable reliability.

Reliability and Test Length

One of the most important influences on test reliability is length. Intuitively, one would not place much credence on the outcome of a one-item test. Chance factors act upon a reader's performance on any single item or task and in a short test this element of chance might bear unduly on the ranking and dispersion of total scores. The test must be sufficiently thorough to allow a fair picture of each reader's capabilities, relative to others, to emerge. Most published tests are of adequate overall length and reliability so that norms based on total raw scores can be applied with confidence. However, some tests can be broken down into separate sub-tests, so that there are special scores for different categories of reading skills. Here, the sub-tests may prove to be of limited reliability. Their results must be treated as suggestive rather than as precise indicators.

Evaluating Reliability – the Standard Error of Measurement

As they stand, reliability coefficients are really only of academic interest. There are few unreliable standardized group reading tests in print and most conventional forms of reading test tasks seem to lend themselves to reliable testing, particularly where answers are scored objectively. In the field of individual oral reading tests, where the test administrator has to judge responses as correct, reliability remains more problematic: it is possible to conceive of a range of chance factors which might influence the tester's judgement from moment to moment. A practical way to explore this is to make a written record of oral reading errors while simultaneously tape-recording the reader. If the initial record shows that the reader has made more than a trivial number of errors the chances are that one or two more will be noted when the tape-recording is played back. Moreover, different teachers may vary in their style of test administration and in their judgement of particular readings/misreadings. Thus an individual test result may depend upon the person giving the test. It can be reasonably hypothesized that if a child were to be given the same test by two different teachers the result would differ in ways that could be attributed to differences between the teachers. In practice this effect may be slight, but it is something than cannot be wholly overlooked, particularly as it is rare for teachers to be given formal training in standard procedures for administering any particular test.

The main use of a reliability coefficient is in deriving the *standard error of measurement* for a test. This is probably the most important of all the statistical concepts in educational testing. If we accept that no test is perfectly reliable, we must also accept that a child's score might differ at least slightly if the test was to be given again on a different occasion or an equivalent form of the test given. The standard error of measurement gives an indication of how great such hypothetical variations would be, taking into account the size of the reliability coefficient.

The standard error can be further conceptualized by imagining the prospect of giving the same test to a child many hundreds of times. This imaginary child is one who never gets bored or tired and manages to forget completely that she or he has done the test the moment each attempt is completed! Even so, one would not expect the child to obtain exactly the same result each time – it is more likely that the scores would cover a range of at least a few points. A 'mini-distribution' of scores would result. It would be sensible to take the average of this distribution as the best estimate of the child's reading ability, but in doing so one would be aware that results of many of the child's efforts lay either side of the overall average. The standard error of measurement provides the best statistical means of estimating this dispersion in points of raw score. The less reliable the test, the larger the standard error of measurement, and the larger this hypothetical dispersion. Only the Utopian perfectly reliable test would have no standard error and the teachers should appreciate that any real-life test score has this element of inexactitude associated with it.

This understanding is, in itself, a valuable aid in evaluating test results, but it is possible to make more direct use of the standard error of measurement. This is done by adopting the concept of 'true' score. It is assumed that each reader must have a true level of ability, i.e. a true position relative to the mean. Because no test is perfectly reliable the obtained result is only a best guess or *estimate* of this true standing. By applying the standard error it is possible to know, with a specified degree of confidence, the margin or range of scores – the 'confidence limits' – in which a true score would probably lie, relative to the child's obtained result. We can be 95 per cent certain that a true score lies within two standard errors above or below an actual score and 99 per cent confident it lies in the range of two and a half standard errors either side of the actual score. That is to say, in only five or one per cent of a set of test results will true ability lie outside the two sets of confidence limits defined above.

There are practical ways in which the concept of standard error of measurement might be used more widely in testing. For example, where test scores are recorded it would be possible to include not only the exact score obtained but the range, at the 95 per cent level of confidence, in which true score lay. Thus for the *GAP Reading Comprehension Test* which has a standard error of 2.76 points of raw score a list of results might read as follows:

Name	Lower limit at 95 per cent level	Actual score	Upper limit at 95 per cent level
Kim	6	12	18
Alex	19	25	31
Ted	24	30	36

Here each child's raw score has been indicated in terms of twice the standard error – rounded to whole numbers. This leads to the expression of *GAP* 'Reading Ages' (see Chapter 5) in terms of three values:

Name	Lowest Probable Reading Age		Obtained Reading Age		Highest Probable Reading Age	
	years	months	years	months	years	months
Kim	7	5	8	1	8	3
Alex	8	4	8	6	8	11
Ted	8	6	8	10	9	5

Such a practice would emphasize to anyone who examined such records that scores on tests, however well standardized, are simply scientific estimates, not eternally fixed values. This becomes particularly important when there is talk of greater public accessibility to educational records. A radical extension of this would be only to record the upper and lower limits of the true score in terms of the standard error of measurement and dispense with actual scores completely.

Validity

It should be apparent that however reliable or well standardized a test may be, this alone does not create sufficient grounds for confidently using it as an indicator of reading ability. How do we know the test is 'really testing reading'? There are many critics of reading tests who would answer this by saying that reading tests only deal with trivial or peripheral aspects of reading. There are certainly many ways of defining reading which make it largely untestable and there are many aspects of reading, such as enjoyment and insight, which are not easily measurable. In effect, reading means different things to different people and different aspects of reading can be covered more or less effectively by different tests. It is thus expecting too much that any one test will meet universal approval as a 'true test of reading'. At the same time, it is self-evident that all reading tests do entail activities which in some sense can be described as 'reading'. Also, test constructors apply certain 'validity' checks to demonstrate that some degree of faith can be placed in the test.

Test validity is usually generally defined as evidence that the test measures what it claims to measure. In the case of reading this might be translated into the requirement that a test should be a dependable basis for making judgements, predictions or general-izations about how well a child will read outside the immediate test situation. There is no one infallible or indisputable way this could be done. However, test constructors often incorporate checks to ensure that their tests are at least on the right lines.

Concurrent Validity

The most common practice is to give children one or more existing reading tests, alongside a new test under development. Where the tests are given close together in time this form of validation is termed *concurrent*. Studies of this sort usually reveal a substantial agreement even where the tests involved appear to vary in content. This could be taken as evidence for the theory that reading is either a general unitary process or composed of closely inter-related processes. It might also be taken to show that all reading tests are on the wrong lines altogether! An alternative

strategy for concurrent validation is to compare teachers' judgements of children's reading ability with test results. Where
teachers are asked to rank children in class order there is usually a
fair degree of agreement with rankings based on test results.
Again, there are two ways of regarding such validation. Is this
evidence of a test's capacity to encapsulate professional judgement, or is it just evidence that tests only tell teachers what they
know already? In fact, the latter scoff is based on a half truth. A
fully standardized test not only ranks children but relates their
performance to a norm – something only widely experienced
teachers could do with any accuracy. There are other considerations. Not all teachers will be sufficiently experienced or familiar
with their children even to rank them with any confidence. There
are also many administrative purposes for testing in which it is
reassuring, if not essential, to know there is some correspondence
between test results and teacher rankings, but where a normative
dimension to results is also needed.

Predictive Validity

Where a substantial period is allowed to elapse between the test
and the measure used to validate it the procedure is termed
'predictive' validation. Studies of this sort are most common in the
development of 'readiness' and screening tests. In such cases the
results of an initial test are followed up some time later with a
measure of actual progress in learning to read. The general
argument here is that a test is valid if it *predicts* future
performance. Generally, the concept of predictive validity is of
limited relevance to reading. Over time, a child's reading
attainment, relative to the norm, may improve or deteriorate for a
range of reasons. These will include quality of teaching, health,
social, domestic and emotional factors. It would thus be naive to
expect anything more than an inexact relationship between an
initial test score and a longer-term criterion of predictive validity.

Face and Content Validity

A plausible way of validating a test is to have a panel of experts –

teachers and reading specialists – vet the format, content and items of the test. The test is then said to have 'face' or 'content' validity: there is an authoritative consensus that it 'looks' as if it is testing reading. Although experts can be wrong there is much to be said for carrying out face validation with reading tests. However, there are few published tests which have been subjected to such scrutiny with any rigour. Evidence for face validity, if mentioned at all, tends to be based on the test author's own, far from objective, judgement. Many published tests have superficial face/content validity in that they involve manipulation of written language. At the same time, few would probably emerge unscathed from a systematic expert analysis, as the critical tone of some reviews in *Review of Reading Tests* (Vincent *et al.*, 1983) attests.

Construct Validity

In the field of psychological measurement it is customary to speak of the processes, areas, traits or dimensions that tests measure as 'constructs'. So far this book has taken for granted the existence of a construct called variously reading 'attainment', 'ability' or 'achievement'. Evidence which supports or illuminates this assumption is said to provide 'construct' validity. Cronbach (1971), in a useful essay on construct validity, says 'Every time an educator asks, "But what does the instrument really measure?", he is calling for information on construct validity'.

A variety of experimental and research procedures can be used to establish construct validity, but in practice constructors of reading tests, if they tackle the problem at all, tend to limit their attention to one or two methods. The most popular of these is to carry out a statistical analysis of relationships between tests. If Reading Test X is found to correlate highly with other reading tests, but not so highly with tests of other skills (e.g. mathematics, verbal reasoning), this may be taken as evidence for the validity of the 'construct' of reading ability and for the construct validity of Test X itself. A similar approach may be adopted with a test composed of separate sub-tests designed to measure different sub-skills of reading. These sub-skills could be regarded as having some individual construct validity if it was found they were not statistically associated with one another. In practice, where studies of this sort are carried out close associations between most postulated sub-skills are usually found, particularly in the field of reading comprehension.

CHAPTER 5

Reading Test Scales

So far, test norms and standards have been referred to in general terms as averages for samples or populations. For these to be applied in the appraisal of individual children's performance it is necessary to derive a scaling system from the results of the standardization trials. This will be presented as a conversion table which equates each possible raw score for the test with some sort of scaled score.

Reading Ages (RAs)

In Britain the most common form of scaled score is the Reading Age (RA). Unfortunately, it is also the most ambiguous and misleading method of scaling reading test scores.

One of the main problems is the variety of possible ways in which an RA scale can be derived. The most typical procedure is to find the score reached by half of a given chronological age (CA) group (the *median* score) and treat that CA as the RA equivalent of the raw score. For example, in Young's *Group Reading Test* approximately half the children of 7.00 years of age scored over 21. Accordingly a score of 21 earns an RA of 7.00 years. It is easy to overlook, however, that this score of 21 was *not* reached by approximately 50 per cent of the pupils. It would be equally reasonable to have examined all the ages of children who scored 21 and establish the mid-point in their age range – i.e. divide the group into equal 'older' and 'younger' halves, taking the dividing point of age as the RA equivalent to a score of 21. However, this might well not coincide with a CA of 7.00.

A further set of reasonable alternatives would be to produce RAs on the basis of arithmetic *means*. This would involve equating mean ages with score groups or mean scores with age groups. Although in practice means are less commonly used in reading age scaling many test users probably assume them to have been the criterion.

A third set of procedures involves equating raw score with RAs on other tests rather than the children's actual CAs. The rationale for this is that a raw score on a newer test can be related directly to the RA the child would have obtained on an established test or a test which would be more time-consuming to give. For example, a raw score of 31 on Young's *Group Reading Test* is 'worth' an RA of 8.00 on the *Salford Sentence Reading Test*. There is a variety of ways in which two tests can be equated for this purpose and, again, different methods will give somewhat different conversion values.

Thus, RAs rest upon one of a number of more or less simple ways in which test scores can be matched with CA or other test scores and the selection of method is arbitrary. Furthermore, many test manuals do not make it at all clear how, exactly, the RAs were derived. Yet in school they are sometimes invested with a meaning and authority out of all proportion to their (perhaps unknown) statistical origins. The reference to age seems to imply something about the level of *development* of a child's reading, as if certain skills and abilities were associated with particular reading ages in an hierarchical progression. In fact, a 7-year-old with a reading age of 7.00 will be very different, as a reader, to an 11-year-old with a reading age of 7.00. The implication that the RA scale is developmental in the sense that physical growth, spoken language acquisition or conceptual thinking may be, is highly questionable. In particular, a child's level of ability in reading will be as much a function of opportunities to learn to read as of CA.

There is a further terminological objection. It is common to speak of children 'with' or 'having' an RA of so many years, just as we do of children's CA. However, strictly speaking, an RA increases with time, albeit in fits and starts rather than contin-uously, like CA. Thus a child's attributed RA is specific to the date of testing and to speak of a child 'having' a particular RA on the strength of a test given some months previously can be misleading.

The expression of test results in units of RA continues to be demanded by many teachers. It seems the powerful fascination of the system remains unabated. (The author has recently heard references to children 'having a Cliff Moon Reading Age of . . .' or simply 'having a Cliff Moon'.) The debate about the merits and deficiencies of the reading age scale can be fully followed up in Vincent (1974) and Bookbinder (1976). To this might be added the (mischievous) suggestion that the next time you hear a colleague refer to a child's reading age you ask him to explain what a reading age is . . .

Reading Quotients (RQs)

It used to be customary to convert reading ages into 'quotients' using the formula $RA/CA \times 100$. It followed that the 'normal' child would earn a quotient of 100, while quotients above or below this indicated relative backwardness or superiority. This procedure does not have any particular merits and has largely fallen into disuse, although the notion that a score of 100 is 'average' or 'normal' has remained.

Standardized Scores

Most modern reading tests include conversion tables which provide separate norms for different age groups in the range for which the test is standardized. Like the old quotient system, the mean for each age group is set at 100. However, scores above or below 100 are interpretable in relation to a hypothetical 'normal curve'. This curve is assumed to reflect or model the distribution of reading ability within each of the age groups to be tested. Early chapters in most introductory textbooks on statistics or educational measurement usually deal with the normal curve and it is worth referring to one or two of these if possible. The most important direct implication of applying the normal curve model is in the way standardized scores are interpreted. Each standardized score indicates how the reader has performed in relation to all the children of the same age – or age band – in the standardization sample. For example, a score of 115 puts the reader above 87 per cent of the sample. This is also the child's estimated position in relation to the population. A standardized score of 100 places the reader above 50 per cent of the sample/population and also corresponds to the mean raw score of the reader's age group. A reader with a standardized score of 100 is thus often spoken of as 'average for his/her age' although, again, this is really just a convention that 'normal equals adequate'. The following table gives more examples:

Standardized Score	Proportion Estimated to Perform Below This Standardized Score
130	98.1
125	95.2
120	90.9
115	84.1
100	50.0
85	15.8
80	9.1
75	4.8
70	2.3

Standardized scores only have meaning in these proportional terms and should not be invested with 'psychological' meaning. For example, a standardized score of 85 is sometimes taken as a criterion of backwardness. It means that the reader is estimated to be above less than sixteen per cent of the age group – and no more than this.

The above reference to 'estimation' is significant. Standardized score tables are produced by examining the general tendency for score to increase with age. On the basis of this trend raw scores and standardized scores are systematically matched up. This involves a certain amount of 'smoothing out' so that there appears to be an orderly and progressive increase in the raw score corresponding with any given standardized score throughout the conversion table. Examine any reading test manual which contains standardized score tables. You will see that the average converted score of 100 corresponds with a raw score which increases for successive age groups. However, this does not mean that the average raw score for any particular age group in the standardization sample corresponded exactly with the tabulated raw score.

The precise obtained value may have been somewhat higher or lower. However, to apply a consistent adjustment for age throughout the table it is necessary to overlook the actual scores of any particular age group and work in terms of general trends. The resulting correspondence between raw and standardized scores is thus an approximation rather than an exact matching with the original results.

Standardized scores certainly have advantages over quotients in relating a child's performance to the average. Backwardness and superiority have a specific meaning in terms of distance from the average. The incorporation of an age adjustment by supplying separate tables to allow a child's score to be compared only with those of the same age is also of some value. However, it is worth recalling that this compensation for age differences originated with eleven-plus testing where it was necessary to avoid bias towards the selection of older children.

Reference is sometimes made to the 'standard deviation' of the standardized score scale. The standard deviation of any test gives an indication of how far the scores are spread out. However, in the standardized score system the standard deviation is 'set' to be 15 points of standardized score and the conversion tables are so prepared that the standard deviation may be interpreted as if it reflected portions of the normal curve. The standard deviation is a useful concept in interpretation of standardized scores but it is probably not so fundamental that it cannot be left to later, subsidiary reading.

Finally, variations in nomenclature should be mentioned. The terms 'standard age scores', 'standardized age-adjusted scores', 'normalized scores', 'standard scores' and indeed 'quotients' are variously used to describe this same system which a) converts raw scores to a scale with a mean of 100 (and a standard deviation of 15), b) is based on the normal curve, and c) is applied according to the child's chronological age in years and months.

Percentiles

It has been explained that standardized scores relate to the percentages of children estimated to score below any particular raw score. The size of these percentages can be expressed more directly as percentile scores. A percentile score indicates the percentage of children below the raw score to which it corresponds. In a standardized test, a percentile score indicates where, in proportional terms, a child stands relative to the population which the test norms reflect. A raw score which earned a percentile score of 50 would be higher than that obtained by 50 per cent of the sample. It would also be equivalent to a standardized score of 100 and standardized scores and percentiles convey very similar information about a reader's performance.

Strictly speaking, a percentile is a point which divides a sample or population; thus a child cannot be placed *at* a percentile, only *in* the percentage above or below a percentile. However, a raw score which is expressed as a percentile *equivalent* indicates the percentage of children *at and below* that raw score. The two types of scales are calculated slightly differently, leading to minor differences. A percentile equivalent corresponding to a particular standardized score will always be slightly greater than the corresponding percentile. For example, the standardized score of 100 has a percentile equivalent of 51.5 – not 50.0 exactly. It is not always clear whether a test is employing a percentile or percentile equivalent scale although in practice the possible differences are unlikely to be of any educational importance.

Other Scales

Some reading test manuals include other scales such as T-scores, and stanines. These are common in the general field of educational and psychological measurement, but are only found occasionally in reading tests. Most such additional scales are simplified versions of standardized scores and percentile scales and do not introduce any new theoretical dimension. For example, the stanine scale (an abbreviation of 'standard-nine') is a simplified grouping of standardized scores into nine categories so that a child's score can vary between 1 and 9 with a score of 5 representing the average grouping around the mean. The T-score scale is somewhat less condensed. It is based on a scale mean of 50 (rather than 100) and a standard deviation of 10 (rather than 15). Thus a standardized score of 85 would be equivalent to a T-score of 40. However, there may be practical advantages in the availability of such scales. For example, there may be occasions on which it is desirable to minimize slight differences between individuals or groups or where it might be misleading to refer to exact standardized scores, and a more general 'grouping' is preferable.

Some reading tests of American origin refer to 'grade equivalent scores'. These are based on norms for children in successive year grades in US schools and could roughly be equated with reading ages by simply adding five to the grade score to give a score in years of RA – although grades are graduated in tenths of a year, not by months. In principle, US grades differ from age groupings in that they refer to a level or stage of schooling, not to chronological age. This might seem a superior measure to RA. However, grade scores have their own problems and ambiguities and in 1982 the International Reading Association passed a resolution condemning their use as a measure of superiority or backwardness in reading. Some of the points made in this resolution (reproduced in *The Reading Teacher,* Vol. 35 No. 3 p. 464) apply equally to the RA scale.

The Rasch Scale

Some recently produced tests employ ability scales based on the 'Rasch' model. Proponents of Rasch-based scales claim that they are closer to measurement in the natural world than other educational test scales. The scales discussed above all related a reader's performance to an average, based on the normal curve. Rasch-based scales seek to express ability in *absolute* terms rather than relative to the normal curve. Full introductions to Rasch analysis can be found in Choppin (1979) and Satterly (1981). As an example, a reader with a standardized score of 140 would not be 'twice as good a reader' as one with a standardized score of 70. Nor is a Reading Age of 14.00 'twice' a RA of 7.00. Test scales based on Rasch analysis aspire to this property. A child with a Rasch score of, say, 60 is said to be 'twice' as able as a child with a score of 30. Similarly, if both children subsequently improve their scores by ten points they could be regarded as having made equal progress. However, this seemingly direct meaning is based on the relative probabilities of readers of given ability passing or failing test items of any particular difficulty. The scale has to be thought of in terms of odds and probabilities, as Satterly (1981) has noted.

CHAPTER 6

Uses and Purposes of Standardized Testing

It *is* possible to keep a class quiet and busy for at least 20 minutes by giving a suitable group reading test. However, incidental benefits of this sort apart, it must be acknowledged that most teachers do not view standardized reading tests with positive interest and enthusiasm. Yet, they continue to use them. As *A Review of Reading Tests* (Vincent *et al.*, 1983) shows, there are numerous standardized tests in print and available to British teachers. This implies the existence of a market for such wares. The statistics presented by the ETSP team suggest that some, at least, are in wide use. They would also suggest that some of the reading tests most highly recommended in the *Review* are hardly used at all.

The full reasons for the continued popularity of standardized reading tests in school are not entirely clear. Their attractions, according to the ETSP research, rest upon their objectivity, neutrality and comparability. They also note that setting tests is a central part of many teachers' work and that published materials in the form of standardized tests provide a ready-made resource. However, an important finding of the ETSP project was that standardized tests were often not used as fruitfully as they might be and that some stated purposes did not match with actual use. This chapter will review some of the main uses to which such tests *can* be put. This provides a rationale and justification for use of standardized testing, and suggests some directions for good practice – even if these are not always common practice. In fact, one of the most substantial problems uncovered by the ETSP project concerned the lack of co-ordination between purpose and outcome of LEA testing programmes rather than the limitations of school-initiated testing. Ways in which practice might be improved at LEA level are clearly indicated in the ETSP report. This chapter is addressed to the problem of making more effective use of standardized tests in school, whether introduced on the school's own initiative or provided by the LEA.

Individual Appraisal: Record Keeping and Transfer Testing

The most obvious and direct use of a reading test is to find out how well an individual child can read. However, the purposes behind this are varied. There are transient and casual uses, such as satisfaction of the teacher's general curiosity about how well a child can read. There are dangers in this 'know your own IQ' use of tests. Standardized testing has numerous serious applications which may be discredited if it is also carried out as a glorified parlour game.

Of the more important serious uses, individual *record keeping* is the most prominent. It is not possible here to go into the larger controversies and issues in school record keeping. However, the inclusion of standardized test scores on record cards is customarily justified in that they provide objective and normative data alongside the more subjective and 'local' perspectives which inevitably feature in a record system. It should be said that if standardized test scores are to be included certain conditions should be observed. The child's age at time of testing and test used should be clearly indicated. The ETSP report expresses reservations about the advisability of placing on record test results which will be used by someone else at a later date when a particular score may no longer be relevant or representative. The report also notes that test results may have been obtained without close observation of standard administration and scoring guidelines. This effect could also call into question the value of standardized testing for cumulative record keeping. Both problems point to the need for professional standards and expertise. If tests are to be used it is essential that they are part of a long-term programme of individual monitoring so that information is annually updated. Also, some rigour and consistency (for example, double marking of tests), must be applied in their administration and marking. This might render testing for record-keeping a more demanding exercise than has often been the case. Moreover, it is highly desirable that the scores should be recorded in terms of the test's standard error of measurement, a key statistical concept described in Chapter 4. This latter precaution should prevent over-literal interpretation of the recorded score, but again, it requires a greater commitment of effort and resources.

A use closely associated with record keeping is the passing on of test results and record forms to other agencies or institutions, particularly when a child changes school – *transfer testing*. The most common instance of this is the transition from Junior to Secondary school. Some tests, such as the *London Reading Test* and the NFER *Transitional Assessment Modules in English,* were specifically designed for this purpose. The ETSP researchers found that the main application of test results was for formation of teaching groups, either in bands, sets or ability groups. The results will also alert secondary remedial teachers to children who will need special help if prior 'screening' (see p.57) has failed to do so. Transfer testing is usually carried out in the Junior school, although some Secondary schools find such diversity of practice – feeder schools use different tests and some do not test at all – that re-testing of all a first-year intake has to be carried out on entry. This also reduces the chance that variations in administration procedure or 'sympathetic' scoring will colour results.

There are clear advantages of comparability and objectivity in obtaining standardized test results for all pupils entering a secondary school from different feeder Junior schools. In view of the observations made earlier about the need for uniformity of test and consistency in administration and scoring, some Secondary schools may be wise to carry out additional testing for themselves.

Even where agreement is reached between Primary and Secondary schools to ensure consistency in all aspects of transfer testing, the provision of test results in isolation on transfer cannot be recommended. These should be, and usually are, accompanied by other forms of assessment – sometimes including samples of work produced by the child. Also, the test results themselves need amplification. Details of the test used and date of testing are needed, together with the 'confidence limits' defined by the standard error of measurement – even at the risk of being irritatingly over-informative. Above all, if the test results seem unrepresentative they should be accompanied by an appropriate comment from a teacher who knows the child. The practice of altering the results (usually upwards) is never defensible.

Results of reading tests are sometimes used in advising parents. The ETSP found many teachers who were unwilling to disclose precise figures to parents although they also present a case study of an LEA where results were made available as a matter of policy. It is difficult to recommend a universal code of practice in this respect (perhaps authors of books about testing reading are more exercised about this than parents or teachers themselves!). Clearly, if a policy of parental acess or disclosure is adopted it is crucial that the teachers themselves have a clear understanding of the precise meaning, limitations and ramifications of standardized test scores. This is essential if they are to communicate accurately and truthfully with parents. Most of the dangers and alleged abuses associated with standardized tests arise from misunderstanding rather than malintent. If a school endorses the view that parents are entitled to details of test results it must also accept the obligation to explain what they mean. This subject is explored a little further in Chapter 12.

Screening

Screening is a term used to describe two kinds of activities:
1. The identification of children who are in danger of encountering future difficulty in reading.
2. The identification of readers who are already experiencing difficulty and are below average for their age.

The first form of screening requires the use of some kind of prognostic device – typically a checklist rather than a standardized test – which assesses conditions which are antecedent to reading difficulty. Potton (1983) provides a useful introduction to such 'speculative' screening. However, his conclusion is that this is a mistaken attempt to apply a 'medical' model of screening to an educational setting.

The second form, which Potton terms 'classificatory' screening, is less contentious. It is concerned with those who have indisputably fallen behind. It is also a purpose to which some standardized tests are particularly well suited. Such statistical features as reliability, normative interpretation of scores and capacity to differentiate between readers of different ability are invaluable if poor readers are to be picked out accurately. It follows that for satisfactory screening a test should have these features.

The general principle behind classificatory screening is to test all children in a school or local authority who are at a critical point in their educational careers, such as transition between levels of schooling. Two sorts of criteria may then be applied. A simple cut-off point may be set, expressed either in units of years of backwardness (the extent to which RA is below CA) or as a standardized score. The precise number of children who would be 'collected' in this way could not be known in advance, and the alternative is to aim to identify a specified percentage of 'lowest scorers'. If resources only allow special help for one per cent of those tested it may be judged expedient to screen for the lowest one per cent. It must be appreciated that neither procedure is infallible and will result in 'false positives' and 'false negatives'. Whatever the cut-off score, there will be children who score at or just below the point set who could have 'true' scores above it. Similarly, there will be children in the 'bottom per cent' group whose 'true' position is above this group. The problem is comparable to that of 'borderline' pass/fail candidates in an exam – some scrape through who 'deserve' to fail and vice versa. The problem is exacerbated by the tendency for test scores to be less reliable at the extremes so that the lower the cut-off score set the more 'hit and miss' the process becomes. In effect, test-based screening needs to be moderated by other considerations, such as teachers' recommendations.

The nature of the selection criterion needs further comment. There are no 'standard' score points or percentages that can be laid down as the 'correct' ones to use, although 18 months' retardation in Reading Age and standardized scores below 85 are probably typical customary criteria. It is also worth reflecting that even if reading standards became dramatically better there would still be children who, on standardized tests, seemed 'backward for their age', simply because standardized tests are designed to spread out and differentiate the children who take them. This problem can be partly overcome by adopting a diagnostic screening criterion. Certain tests, such as the *Aston Index* and the *Bangor Dyslexia Test* claim to do this by revealing patterns of test performance indicative of specified reading difficulty. Such tests may focus on particular types of poor readers but they are probably not a comprehensive solution to the problem of identifying all children who genuinely need extra help with reading. Ideally, screening should be based on tests which deal with mastery of essential reading skills appropriate to the age group tested – a criterion-referenced approach. Few tests of this sort are available, although the principles of criterion-referenced testing are discussed further in Chapter 8.

Finally, it must be noted that the ETSP report expressed some doubts over the integration of LEA-wide screening programmes and arrangements for remedial intervention and provision. Clearly, it is no use forming remedial groups prior to giving a screening test if there is insufficient flexibility to make remedial provision for additional or different children subsequently. The danger that testing becomes a substitute, rather than a guide, for action must be seriously considered.

Monitoring

Closely allied to screening is the practice of monitoring – the long-term and regular use of standardized testing. In fact, monitoring is a general term which applies to a number of uses, but recurrent screening, re-testing of children at various points throughout a school career, is one of the most common forms of monitoring. Indeed, given the fallibility of testing, successive checking in this way is highly desirable to identify children who previously slipped through the net, or those who have more recently started to fall behind in their reading. This may seem to call for a great deal of testing. However, if monitoring is based on a quickly administered and marked group test, such as NFER Tests A, AB, or BD or Young's *Group Reading Test,* the actual amount of inconvenience is modest. At the same time it must be admitted that more searching tests, such as the *Edinburgh Reading Tests* series, would be a superior choice.

The term 'monitoring' also refers to programmes of testing

involving successive groups of different children at particular ages. The purpose of such monitoring is to observe the overall trend in standards of reading over time. The most highly developed example is the national language monitoring programme carried out by the Assessment of Performance Unit (APU) of the DES. The work of the APU itself is discussed in Chapter 10. However, many LEAs conduct similar exercises by annually testing particular age groups. The results of such surveys may be used in local public debates about 'standards' in schools and, less publicly, to observe differences in average performance of individual schools. Unlike the APU which samples small proportions of national age group populations, LEAs usually 'blanket test' all the children in the population in an age group. In this way, monitoring can double up as a screening exercise although critics, for reasons which are rarely well explained, sometimes regard this as excessive testing of children.

Monitoring of children is undeniably a politically-charged activity, and many critics of national monitoring by APU have detected sinister intentions. At LEA level tests have featured in controversial enquiries into standards and one Chief Education Officer was reported in *The Times Educational Supplement* (2.12.83) as proposing to use tests to detect incompetent teachers. Nevertheless, it would seem that fears over use of standardized tests by LEAs as instruments of direct or 'punitive' accountability have been exaggerated. The ETSP researchers certainly found no evidence for this. In any case, the problem of distinguishing between good and bad teachers of reading is a complicated one, as Gray (1979) has shown. It is hard to believe anyone would make serious use of tests for such a purpose. Perhaps the greatest criticism that can be levelled at monitoring through standardized tests is that very little use of any sort is made of the results. Russell (1970) was able to report positive action as result of reading surveys carried out in the ILEA. However, on the basis of their national analysis of LEA monitoring ten years later ETSP express concern that while monitoring may continue it is uncertain that resources are any longer available to act upon results.

Unfortunately this negative connotation of testing – be it genuine or alleged – has obscured potential positive values of monitoring, particularly when initiated by individual schools as a form of self-evaluation. Test results can add objective evidence to what is all too often a subjective debate. Alarmists can speak of 'falling standards of literacy' with a hysteria suggesting an imminent collapse of culture and civilization. The availability of test results to temporize such emotion is, surely, beneficial. Schools which carry out effective internal monitoring will, at worst, have a discrete early warning of the need to pay more attention to reading and, at best, valuable evidence of their continuing efficiency. The ETSP report certainly makes a number of passing references to schools which appear to be using regular testing for such 'defensive' or 'strategic' ends.

Monitoring, particularly in the way adopted by APU, is fraught with technical difficulties. However, these centre upon the use of Rasch analysis to select or exclude items and for re-stocking the 'bank' of items with fresh materials over time. It does not follow that more efficient self-monitoring could not be carried out by schools and some guidelines for this can be suggested. For example, certain consistencies have to be observed in the time of year of testing, age groups tested and the test used for monitoring. A well-standardized test must be used if performance or improvement is to be evaluated in relation to a specified norm. The norms used must be appropriate to the age and year group, and, ideally, time of year of testing. A test originally standardized for top Juniors in the summer term will be 'pessimistic' if used at the beginning of the year. Some knowledge of elementary statistics is also desirable if each year's results are to be summarized and interpreted correctly. However, the widespread availability of microcomputers makes the actual storage and analysis of test results a matter of simple routine.

Grouping

A further extension of screening is the use of test scores as a basis for grouping children, particularly into remedial reading groups. The intention behind this, of ensuring that help goes to those who most need it, is laudable. At the same time, there are certain dangers. Children who are equally 'backward' will not necessarily have the same kinds of difficulties or need the same kinds of help, particularly where there are chronological age differences. The principle of 'which children', not 'what teaching' applies generally to grouping readers on the basis of test results. For example, it is rarely possible to 'match' levels of reading material with levels of reading attainment. The ETSP reported that a substantial number of class teachers regarded test results as a basis for placement on reading schemes. Unfortunately the report does not enlarge upon this finding but it would seem to be a questionable practice. Few, if any, published tests or reading schemes are designed for use in this way. A great deal of research would be needed to establish reliable ways of doing this. Similarly, although the 'readability' of books can be expressed as a reading age, this has no direct relevance to RAs based on test results. The reading age of a book and the reading age of a child are, at best, tenuously related. (Useful introductions to readability are provided by Gilliland, 1972, and Harrison, 1980).

Assessing Progress and Improvement

It would seem sensible, having initially established a child's reading ability, to carry out subsequent testing to check that progress remains satisfactory or that desired improvement has been made. The terms 'progress' and 'improvement' have some-what different implications – although the practical problems they raise are similar. The monitoring of progress is usually closely related to school-wide record keeping and will be part of a general policy of keeping an unobtrusive check on children's educational development. It reflects the teacher's concern that things *remain* more or less normal. By contrast, assessment of improvement refers to remedial purposes and situations in which the teacher is concerned to bring about additional progress because the level of reading is less than 'normal' to start with.

In their simplest forms both purposes involve giving the same test more than once, for example on an annual basis. There are obvious disadvantages in giving the same test twice. For example, if the time between initial and follow-up testing is short, then the influence of immediate recall of answers previously given cannot be discounted, nor can the possible effects of recent practice of taking tests in the particular form used. More seriously, the spurious effect of 'regression to the mean' needs to be considered. This can happen when readers who perform at the extremes covered by the test – very good or very poor readers – are re-tested. It is possible that some extreme cases will score somewhat closer to the test mean, i.e. higher or lower, on re-testing, even though no real improvement, or deterioration, has taken place. This effect can be explained theoretically in terms of test unreliability – which will be greatest at the extremes. However, a non-technical way of putting it would be to say that for poor readers there is 'no way to change but up' and for good readers there is 'no way to change but down'! This effect has practical implications for monitoring progress of poor readers. It is easy to take spurious test improvement due to regression to the mean as a sign that a child has made real progress. This can be avoided by using an 'easy' test which allows the poor reader to gain an initial score nearer to the mean. This will provide a more reliable baseline to measure subsequent progress. It would also be essential to look for 'non-test' criteria of improvement. If the *only* sign of progress is a modest increment in test score the result should be treated with scepticism.

There is no doubt that many children are tested far too frequently. For general monitoring of normal progress stand-ardized testing need only be carried out annually. The practice of giving the same test twice yearly, or more often, is probably counterproductive, particularly as such over-testing usually involves the least satisfactory oral word recognition tests. If some special intervention programme has been introduced with the aim of achieving additional progress then it may be appropriate to test more frequently. Nevertheless, the understandable temptation repeatedly to test children in remedial groups in a desperate search for the slightest glimmer of improvement should be resisted!

It has already been noted that some standardized tests are prepared in equivalent or parallel forms. This clearly is an aid to measuring progress and eliminates the problem of specific recall. Ideally, such parallel forms should build in an adjustment for practice in the sense mentioned above. However, amongst generally available tests only the NFER-Nelson *Wide-span* includes such a refinement. (Occasionally the claim to be parallel is itself misleading. Form C of the *Neale Analysis of Reading Ability,* for example, is probably harder than forms A and B).

A variation on the provision of parallel forms is the creation of multi-level tests in a graded series. The *Primary Reading Test,* for example, comes in two overlapping levels, as well as parallel forms. Level 1 is designed to cover the range of performance of top Infants to second year Juniors, while Level 2 is intended for the middle to top Junior range. An even more thorough solution is to produce separate tests to cover successive age groups, as in the *Hunter-Grundin Literacy Profiles* or the *Edinburgh Reading Tests*. For a school genuinely committed to careful monitoring of progress, test series of this sort would be the best solution.

One of the most crucial aspects of measuring progress is the form in which the measurement is expressed. Probably, the most widespread practice is to talk in terms of gain in 'reading age'. In spite of the intuitive appeal of the RA scale it can easily be misinterpreted. The main reservations surrounding the RA scale have already been reviewed, but no apology is made for rehearsing them here.

Unlike units of chronological age, such as years and months, units of RA are not necessarily equal or additive. A year's increase in reading age is not 'twice' as much improvement as six months' progress. Nor can it be assumed that a ten-year-old who makes a year's progress has made the 'same' amount of progress as a seven-year-old who has also gained a year in the same amount of time. All that can be said of a gain in RA is that a reader who formerly obtained a test score which in some sense was typical of age group A has now earned a score typical of age group B.

Expression of progress in points of standardized score is perhaps less prone to misunderstanding, although it seems more remote from real life than units of years or months. A change in a reader's standardized score represents directly a change in the reader's position relative to others of the same age group. Although seemingly less informative than improvement expressed in reading age terms this is certainly less ambiguous.

Neither of the above systems, nor indeed any reading test scale which is related to norms and averages, says anything about *what* a reader has learned. This is easily overlooked in the case of reading ages. The real differences between average or typical children of different ages are qualitative and quite apparent to a teacher. However, it does not follow that because we know what an average eight-year-old can do that we know, in operational terms, what an RA of eight years means. A 16-year-old with an RA of 8.00 will be a very different sort of reader from a 7-year-old with such a reading age!

There is a further limitation to norm-based reading tests as a means of assessing progress. Test norms are established by giving a test to a large number of children of different ages at the same time. The increase in raw score across successive age groups is taken as an indication of the normal progress readers would make over the period represented by the age differences between groups. The image of 'normal' progress which thus emerges is one of a steady and regular increase in raw score test performance as a child gets older. This takes no account of the possibility that in general children's rate of progress is varied in rate over a school year. A number of research studies have uncovered 'seasonal effects' whereby rate of increase varies with the time of year. Nor do test norms take account of the possibility that even 'normal' children will differ in their rate of progress. Normal progress is more likely to be in fits and starts rather than regular monthly increments, as implied by standardized tests. In effect, stand-ardized tests give norms for group 'performance' at different ages (as established at the particular time of year when the tests were given), not norms for individual *progress* throughout a school year. The expectations set up by test norms must therefore not be taken at face value. Certain tests, such as the *Wide-span* and the *London Reading Test* are standardized in a way which at least partly compensates for differences associated with the time of testing. However, the question of long-term individual progress remains largely neglected by test producers.

Appraisal of progress or improvement can be taken to a further and more technical stage. This involves the application of statistical tests to determine whether a change or difference between two or more sets of reading tests scores has simply been due to chance fluctuations, or whether it is possible that some more 'genuine' change has really occurred. Such refinements are rarely necessary in the course of normal progress testing, where test data are primarily used as a check on professional judgements made on the basis of having taught a child. However, they are of greater potential importance when the teacher is concerned with effecting improvement. Here the teacher may feel it necessary to provide some checks on 'wishful thinking' – is the result really just due to chance or the unreliability of the test? The problem of imperfect test reliability has already been discussed (Chapter 4).

One ramification of test (un)reliability is that apparent differences between two sets of scores may be compounded of genuine change and chance variations. There is no way of eliminating this possibility with one hundred per cent certainty. However, there are checks which might be considered by a teacher who is concerned to make a more thorough check. For example, Satterly (1981, Chapter 6) describes a way of evaluating two scores against the *standard error of difference*. Where the teacher wishes to check whether readers, as a group, have improved, a *t-test for correlated means* (not to be confused with the T-score scale mentioned previously) can be applied. This tests the hypothesis that the difference between the averages in two sets of scores for the same children is really due to chance. The mechanical steps for using this procedure are described in introductory tests such as Crocker (1981). A less statistically precise graphical procedure is outlined in Vincent and Cresswell (1976, Chapter 6).

Such procedures must be recommended with reservation. Introductory textbooks present an apparent 'orthodoxy' of techniques for comparing sets of test scores. This conceals the extent to which the use of statistics in educational settings remains problematic – particularly in the area of assessing improvement. It has been argued that standardized testing should have a supplementary or confirmatory role in assessment. A similar caution should be attached to statistical analysis. Such criteria should not be applied blindly. For example, if the teacher is satisfied that the possibility of regression to the mean – described previously – can be discounted, and all the children obtain increased test scores and it is possible to verify improvement by other criteria, statistical analysis may be unnecessary. Above all, statistical procedures cannot provide ultimate proof that an improvement has been achieved. They are simply ways of estimating the probability that a change or difference in scores is merely due to chance.

In-School Evaluation

There are various potential uses for standardized tests which remain largely unexplored by schools. The most interesting of these lie in the general area of evaluation and planning. The evidence of the ETSP research is that few schools employ test results to appraise established or new aspects of their work or as a guide to future developments.

Before considering the role of tests in evaluation some comment on in-school evaluation in general is needed. Many teachers would agree, in principle, that it would be worthwhile to scrutinize, formally or consciously, certain – or all – aspects of their own practice. They might also express considerable reservations at the prospect of this being done by people or agencies external to their schools. At the same time, the amount of in-school evaluation which takes place is probably limited. It is most likely to happen when a teacher decides to carry out some form of evaluation to meet the assessment requirements of an award-bearing in-service course. Whatever the actual extent of teacher-initiated evaluation, this does not diminish the case for it to be regarded as a legitimate professional activity.

The position of tests in evaluation is by no means a simple one. In practice, many large-scale evaluation studies of methods and materials for teaching reading have relied heavily on standardized test results. Also, many conventional textbooks on evaluation, particularly those by American authors, treat testing as one of the main tools of the evaluator. In very simple terms, traditional evaluation has involved the use of an 'experimental' approach in which the effects of certain treatments, methods or experiences are assessed. This entails forming experimental and 'control' groups. The former will undergo the special materials or methods while the latter do not. The groups are tested before and after teaching so that any extra learning associated with the special 'treatment' undergone by the experimental group can be identified. When it comes to real-life situations in which teachers wish to evaluate changes in their own practice the problem of designing suitable controls becomes much more complicated. Here the applicability of strict experimental methods is open to question. Critics of the experimental approach to evaluation have argued that much more emphasis should be placed on observation, participation and dialogue with all those involved in the process under evaluation. Thus the evaluator works more like a journalist or anthropologist than a laboratory scientist.

It would be as well to recall that these arguments over evaluation methods tend to be at the level of generality. There are certainly many features of a school's work which certainly do not lend themselves to experimental evaluation, yet it would be rash to claim that no aspects of the teaching of reading lend themselves to experimental or test-based appraisal. Indeed, with suitable technical advice on design and statistical interpretation, quite sophisticated exercises can be carried out. Nor are different methods of evaluation incompatible. Gregory *et al.* (1982) present an excellent example of a study in which various methods, including standardized testing, were used to evaluate the use of remedial reading materials in school. Two practical guides to evaluation in school have been provided by Shipman (1979 and 1983). These adopt an eclectic approach and present the teacher with a range of evaluative strategies, including standardized assessment.

At a more mundane and low-keyed level, standardized test results might contribute to general self-scrutiny. Routine testing not only shows how children are progressing but reflects upon one's own efforts. The problem for the teacher is one of how exactly to involve such data in the process of self-reflection.

To tease out the relationships between pupil performance and effective teaching is a complicated business which continues to exercise the minds of many professional researchers. Researchers may be in the fortunate position of being able to put off any categorical pronouncements about the teaching of reading indefinitely – there is always a case for 'more research'. Teachers themselves are faced with having to make immediate real-life decisions about their own pupils and teaching methods. How effectively this can take account of test results will depend upon the teacher's level of knowledge. To start with, the limitations of reliability, validity, norms and content need to be set against the teacher's knowledge of the children. Only then is it possible to define results which are indicative of success and those which should cause concern. Even then, judgements should be made tentatively and take account of as much other external and additional evidence as possible. If possible, the process should be discussed with a sympathetic colleague who may be able to provide a rational and objective perspective on what one is doing. The need for some aid to distance oneself in some way seems to be important. The ETSP presents a case study of a teacher who, while endeavouring to respond constructively to the implications of recent test results, effectively initiated an entirely nonsensical course of action. Laying open the proposed course of action before professional colleagues – if this had been possible – might have resulted in a more sensible outcome.

One further issue in testing and evaluation is that of test content. If the level of language tested or the mode (oral/silent) does not match the teachers' aims, the subsequent results will be misleading – perhaps disappointing. The need for content of testing and content of teaching to be matched has been mentioned in Chapter 1. Yet it has been found in the course of many research studies that reading tests of seemingly different form and content nevertheless agree with each other substantially. It might therefore appear to follow that it really does not matter what test is used to evaluate an aspect of one's work as 'they all measure roughly the same thing'. This is too glib, particularly if a test is to be used to measure an aspect of reading which has been especially highlighted in teaching – such as evaluative and critical responding to what has been read. A general tendency to agree amongst tests does not mean that the processes measured are identical. It may be that much of this agreement - which is rarely perfect in any case - reflects the reader's capacity to draw upon a general 'reserve' of reading ability in a range of contexts. Efforts to develop proficiency in particular activities, while still partly dependent on the extent of each reader's general ability, might well lead to worthwhile progress in this particular aspect of reading. At this point 'any old test' would not necessarily be sensitive to this difference. This in turn raises another problem – the restriction in the range of aspects of reading covered by standardized tests. It is possible to think of many important aspects of reading which are not adequately tapped by published tests. In fact, reflection may reveal that the need for a normative element is not indispensable. It may be enough to show that pupils have made considerable progress in raw score on a purpose-devised test. The possibilities for such 'teacher made tests' are discussed further in Chapter 12.

CHAPTER 7

Diagnostic Tests and Techniques

Previous chapters have been concerned with assessment of reading attainment. This is primarily a test-based activity. However, in the field of diagnostic assessment the position of published tests, although there are many for this purpose, is not necessarily so central. The experience and clinical judgement of the teacher is of at least equal importance. Many skilled diagnosticians do not resort at all to published materials but prefer to use either materials of their own making, structured techniques or their judgement, based on experience. Those who do use published tests may well only employ them as part of their approach to diagnosis. Accordingly, the latter part of this chapter will consider certain non-test aids to diagnosis, as well as set-piece test materials.

The term 'diagnosis' needs some comment. When used in a remedial context it usually refers to the identification of possible causes of reading difficulty. However, the way in which these difficulties are conceptualized varies greatly. For example, diagnosis may be concerned with underlying cognitive and perceptual weaknesses which act as obstacles to learning or, more simply, with weaknesses in word attack and phonic skills which need to be remedied. Even within these two sub-categories a wide choice of techniques and materials will be encountered. 'Diagnosis' is also used in a number of further senses. These include the assessment of reading 'readiness', the appraisal of strengths and weaknesses in 'higher order' comprehension skills amongst upper Junior or Secondary pupils, the analysis of 'miscues' made during oral reading and assessment of a reader's capacity to deal with texts of a particular level of readability.

There is certainly no single 'correct' orthodoxy in diagnostic assessment. Rather, there is a range of models or approaches. These reflect different theories about reading and the different problems for which diagnostic approaches have been developed. This chapter reviews a representative cross section of some of the main examples.

IQ – Attainment Test Discrepancies: Slow Learners *VS* Under-achievers

A long-established form of diagnostic assessment has been the use of a 'battery', i.e. a set, of standardized tests, including measures of reading and intelligence. The purpose behind such testing is to discriminate between poor readers who are equally poor in measures of general mental ability (IQ), and those who obtain mental test scores which are much higher than those for reading. Those who were uniformly low on all measures would be regarded as 'slow learners' who were probably doing as well at reading as could be expected, given the limits to their intelligence. By contrast, those with relatively high general intelligence might be suffering from some specific handicap which causes their 'under-achievement'. The process of diagnosis is thus one of determining into which of these two categories a reader fits, with the implication that he or she would thereafter need different kinds of help. The 'slow learner' would need patient and carefully structured step-by-step teaching, while the underachiever might well need further diagnosis.

This conception of diagnosis is probably much less widely accepted than formerly. The assumption that an IQ test necessarily indicates reading potential is open to challenge on a number of counts. The evidence that 'Non-Verbal' IQ tests, those which involve the solution of problems presented symbolically or pictorially, are a valid predictor of how well a child should be able to read, is weak. Furthermore, 'Verbal Reasoning' tests which require solution of problems presented in a linguistic mode may not be relevant either. If presented in printed form they clearly penalize poor readers from the outset. The findings of an individual orally administered test may be of greater relevance in distinguishing between different types of poor readers. However, the increasing theoretical objections to the concept of IQ (e.g. Kamin 1974, Evans and Waites 1981) must not be overlooked. One critic who has developed a positive alternative is Stott (1978) who argues that it is much more useful to appraise poor learners in terms of the way they approach learning tasks rather than in terms of their IQ. Stott has devised a checklist, the *Stott Guide to Children's Learning Skills* (Stott, Green and Francis, 1982) which itemizes possible respects in which a child displays faulty approaches to learning. A Preliminary Guide of seven items provides a rapid basis for screening. This deals with the presence of positive learning skills, e.g. 'shows by his answers that he is giving attention'. A Full Guide of 14 items deals with poor learning more fully, e.g. 'looks for ways of evading learning tasks' 'is easily distracted'. The items are completed by the teacher, who must indicate the extent to which each statement applies to the child being assessed. This has the advantage of drawing direct attention to causes of general educational difficulty, of which reading problems may be simply symptomatic.

There is some evidence for the value of the Preliminary Guide as a predictor of reading progress (Green and Francis, 1980; Stott *et al.,* 1983) which would support its adoption as a screening device. The possibility of using the Guide as an alternative to traditional IQ tests and the 'underachiever' *vs.* 'slow learner' distinction is also worth exploring. Faulty approaches to learning are likely to hinder reading progress, regardless of the 'intelligence' of the learner.

Finally it is worth referring to the difficulties encountered by the Assessment of Performance Unit (APU) in tackling the issue of 'underachievement'. One of the four main aims of this DES-based organization was to 'identify significant differences of achievement related to the circumstances in which children learn, including the incidence of underachievement . . .' However, as Gipps and Goldstein (1983) show in their independent evaluation of APU, the Unit failed to achieve this task in spite of the considerable resources and expertise at its disposal.

Readiness Testing

The earliest diagnostic test a reader is likely to encounter would be some form of reading 'readiness' test. The concept of reading readiness owes much to research into children's general mental development, which has studied how concepts are acquired and perceptual abilities evolve. Much of this research showed that young children progress through various 'stages' of mental growth and that the intellectual tasks a child can perform will depend upon the stage reached. It thus seemed reasonable to expect that certain levels of mental development would be essential for learning to read. More specifically, prerequisite thresholds of visual, auditory and conceptual ability would have to be reached if a child was to learn to relate sounds, symbols and meaning. Established tests of reading readiness such as the *Harrison-Stroud Reading Readiness Profiles* and the *Thackray Reading Readiness Profiles* provide, respectively, American and British examples of this approach.

The validity of such tests rests upon their capacity to predict the extent of subsequent progress in learning to read. However, prediction and teaching are not the same thing. It does not follow that the content of a test which is effective in predicting success will provide a useful guide to what is to be taught. A prime example of this is the *Marianne Frostig Developmental Test of Visual Perception.* This test covers a number of visual and motor skills and research seemed to show that poor performance on these tasks was associated with later difficulty in reading. Nevertheless, results of special remedial training material designed to develop the skills measured by the test have been disappointing. It did not appear that additional work on the skills measured by the test 'carried over' into real reading. Thus, most readiness tests are probably best regarded as screening devices which may identify symptoms, but not causes, of potential reading difficulty.

Some reading specialists now emphasize the early conceptual problems young children may have in appreciating the actual nature and purpose of written language. Some newer tests, notably Downing's *Linguistic Awareness in Reading Readiness (LARR)* and some of the test and procedures devised by Marie Clay in *The Early Detection of Reading Difficulties,* focus upon the child's grasp of such concepts as 'letter', 'word' and 'sentence' and the directional nature of print. *LARR* is also particularly concerned with how far the child realizes the communicative function of written language. The formal evidence for the validity of such tests is limited. Nevertheless, they would appear to have great potential for identifying those children who come to school mystified as to the fundamental nature and purpose of literacy as a means of recording and sharing meaning. Such children may well see reading as no more than a competitive ascent through the reading scheme which brings no reward other than teacher and parental approval. Such readiness tests may also be valuable in drawing the teacher's attention to the need of such children to experience stories and books as opposed to perceptual training programmes.

Two final points should be considered before leaving reading readiness. Firstly, it must be acknowledged that the assessment of early reading involves a multitude of matters beyond the scope of any test. The teacher needs to consider how, if at all, results from reading readiness tests might be set alongside, for example, information about social and emotional development and linguistic background. Secondly, the practical problems of testing children so early in their school careers should be mentioned. There are certainly many infant level teachers who feel it would impose excessive stress or demands upon concentration to employ any formal test with their children. Such teachers need to be free to employ reading readiness tests selectively, at their discretion. However, there is a possible danger in prejudging what children will be capable of. This is not always a valid substitute for actually trying materials or tasks out. It should not be overlooked that a properly developed test will have undergone preliminary trials for suitability with the age range for which it is intended. Also, the finding of the HMI primary survey (DES 1976), that some teachers fail to provide reading tasks which match up to the capabilities of more able readers, may be pertinent. This survey also found that it was 'very rare for children in any age or ability to be required to undertake work which was too difficult for them.' Where there was a mismatch between task and learner it was usually a case of the work being too easy. This may imply a tendency towards over-protectiveness amongst some teachers.

Phonic Testing

Much remedial teaching is concerned with developing word recognition and decoding skills. It is therefore hardly surprising that many of the published materials designed for diagnosis of reading difficulty deal with phonic knowledge and blending skill.

Individual phonic tests most commonly take the form of a set of simple word lists containing words which have been selected to cover systematically the major phonic elements. Stephen Jackson's *Get Reading Right,* for example, consists of eleven Phonic Skills tests, each printed on a separate sheet. These display lists of letters or words representing various phonic elements:

1–4. letter names and sounds
   5. blending two and three letter words
   6. final consonant blends and silent 'e'
   7. initial consonant blends
   8. vowel digraphs
   9. consonant digraphs and silent letters
 10. word endings
 11. multi-syllabic words.

The first two tests are group tests, but the remainder are individual oral tests in which the pupil must attempt to read the words displayed on the sheets. The tests to be given to any particular reader are selected according to the judgement of the teacher – testing may be discontinued once sufficient mistakes have been made to furnish material for a number of lessons. A handbook is provided which contains practical suggestions for remedial activities. *Get Reading Right* is a standard and proven example of an individual phonic test which has been in use – perhaps widely – for about ten years. There are more elaborate examples. The *Domain Phonic Test and Workshop* is more exhaustive in its coverage of phonic elements while the *Macmillan Diagnostic Reading Pack* includes phonic tests in an ingenious system of testing based on flow charts which guide the teacher to select appropriate tests. No statistical validation or norms are presented with these, or indeed, with most other individual phonic tests. They must be regarded as practical teaching devices which suggest lines for immediate action but do not claim to uncover possible causes of reading failure other than difficulty in blending and decoding. In fact, although they are presented in published form as tests they do not otherwise greatly differ from the informal phonic checklists teachers devise for themselves or which are sometimes presented in general texts on reading such as Raban's *Phonic Checklist Record Form* (Raban, 1983), Cotterell's *Checklist of Basic Sounds* (Cotterell, 1973) or the phonic tests in Hughes (1975). There is certainly no evidence that they differ from informal examples in what they measure or the accuracy with which they do so. Their main advantage is convenience.

Some test constructors have endeavoured to produce standardized group tests of phonics. By definition this is a difficult task, as group tests need to be silent while phonic teaching involves overt oral behaviour. The *Swansea Test of Phonic Skills* and Carver's *Word Recognition Test* tackle the problem through a multiple-choice technique whereby the reader must match a word spoken by the teacher with its corresponding written form in a set of five printed alternatives. Whether these tests would lead to the same analysis of a reader's phonic skills as an individual oral test has not been investigated. The Swansea test is also interesting in that it uses nonsense words to test phonic knowledge. This eliminates the chance that a word has been correctly read because it is part of the reader's sight vocabulary, rather than because the reader has really mastered the phonic features it represents. Athey (1978) presents evidence to suggest that performance on one of the phonic sub-tests of the *Standard Reading Tests* (Test 7B) could be affected by sight knowledge of the words used.

It would be generally agreed that remedial teaching needs to be carefully structured and, traditionally, phonics has provided this structure. However, fluent readers make use of a range of features of written language in addition to their knowledge of sound-symbol correspondence. Words which cannot be read in isolation on test lists may be read without trouble in the context of a sentence or paragraph. For fluent readers it is only when other features of language are no help that phonic decoding will be employed at all, as for example, the reading of an unfamiliar place name. Although it is possible to be seemingly thorough in assessing phonic weaknesses it must be appreciated that this would still only constitute a partial diagnosis. The teacher would need to know, for example, whether the reader could make use of either grammatical or semantic cues or had developed a capacity for self-correction. These can only be assessed through oral reading of continuous prose, and may well involve some analysis of the 'miscues' exhibited – a technique examined later in this chapter.

Comprehension Skills: Diagnostic Profiles

One of the most important watersheds in the development of a child's reading is that at which reading becomes predominantly a silent and private phenomenon rather than an oral and public one. Most reputable books, research and curriculum projects and courses on the teaching of reading treat it as a continuing learning task well beyond the first two or three years of schooling. Many reading specialists would also question the assumption that just because reading has become a more or less silent act it is no longer a teaching responsibility. It also continues to be a source of difficulty for some children who may well have mastered phonic decoding skills but have failed to develop comprehension or 'higher order' reading skills. Where it is known that the reader's first language is not English, poor comprehension relative to oral accuracy will alert the teacher to the need for general language extension. However, with the exception of ESL readers, to know that a child is poor at comprehension does not, of itself, seem to be a particularly diagnostic piece of information. Accordingly, there have been a number of attempts to produce tests designed to produce a 'profile' of those particular aspects of comprehension in which the reader is weakest.

The fundamental assumption underlying this approach is that reading comprehension is composed of a series of processes or skills, rather in the way psychologists have conceived human intelligence to be composed. The distinction between verbal and non-verbal reasoning ability, for example, has already been referred to. The best-known example of such a breakdown of reading into comprehension subskills is Barrett's Taxonomy (see Clymer 1972) which makes a detailed analysis of subskills under five major headings:

Literal comprehension
Reorganization
Inferential comprehension
Evaluation
Appreciation.

This particular example has, perhaps, monopolized the attention of British teachers and, for reasons to be discussed below, it may have come to be regarded with undue reverence. Nevertheless, it still clearly illustrates the process of analysing reading comprehension into constituent elements or subskills.

It so happens that there is no pure example of a reading test based exactly on Barrett's Taxonomy, although the London Reading Test uses its main categories. However, the general approach is reflected in a number of published tests which incorporate a set or 'battery' of tests or sub-tests designed to assess the supposed processes or component skills. Tests for this purpose are usually standardized and subjected to validity and reliability analyses on the lines described in Chapters 3 and 4. The total raw score will be convertable to an overall attainment score in the usual way. In addition, sub-tests scores will also be convertable to a normative scale. A reader's performance on these tests can thus be recorded in some form of bar chart or graph to permit comparisons and the identification of particular strengths or weaknesses. This, it is argued, can form the basis for follow-up teaching.

The development of tests of this sort has a long history in the USA, although few of these tests have become available in the UK. The best-known versions of British origin are the NFER *EH1, EH2* and *EH3* tests for secondary pupils and the *Edinburgh Reading Tests*. The NFER tests deal respectively with Vocabulary, Comprehension and Rate and can be regarded as a crude example. The Edinburgh series is more elaborate. There are four separate tests, designed for successive age bands between 7.00 and 16.00 years. These contain the following sub-tests:

Stage 1   Vocabulary
             Syntax
             Sequences
             Comprehension

Stage 2   Vocabulary
Comprehension of Sequences
Use of Context
Reading Rate
Comprehension of Essential Ideas

Stage 3   Reading for Facts
Comprehension of Sequences
Retention of Main Ideas
Comprehension of Points of View
Vocabulary

Stage 4   Skimming
Vocabulary
Reading for Facts
Points of View
Comprehension.

Two problems are immediately evident in the above list. 'Comprehension' appears in Stages 1 and 4 alongside more specific definitions of itself. Also, it is hard to discern any rational progression of reading development across the four stages.

Furthermore, the constructors of the Edinburgh tests encountered a problem which has beset many researchers into reading comprehension. Perusal of the test manuals reveals that for the most part the sub-tests are closely correlated. This means that a child's performance will be roughly uniform across sub-tests. Most children will perform equally well or poorly on all the sub-tests and few, if any, children will be genuinely weaker or stronger at particular skills. This is a common finding in research into reading comprehension. Researchers will set out to validate a particular analysis of reading into seemingly separate processes, only to find that many, if not all, of these are closely associated with one another. This in turn leads to the conclusion that comprehension may be a 'unitary' rather than multi-faceted ability. Lunzer and Gardner (1979) include an account of a typical study which leads to this conclusion.

Such findings do not entirely discredit the existence of component processes in reading comprehension. At the least, they may still be said to 'exist' in the sense that it is possible to devise test tasks which seemingly involve or elicit their use. It may be sensible to think of them as separate activities which are closely related and which are also manifestations of a more general underlying reading ability. However, the need for caution – if not scepticism – in examining the claimed validity of any particular taxonomy or theoretical analysis of comprehension sub-skills should be clear. The scope for diagnostic assessment of reading beyond the level of phonics and word recognition using standardized tests remains extremely limited. The available empirical evidence does not suggest that the production of profiles based on sub-test scores would be at all fruitful with any of the tests that have so far been devised.

Are theories or taxonomies which claim to differentiate reading comprehension skills completely invalid? This would be an extreme position. As a general stimulus to thought about the need for breadth in the reading curriculum they can be of value. Moreover, they provide a means of ensuring balance in the choice of items in a standardized attainment test. The *London Reading Test* items, for example, were written in accordance with the main categories in Barrett's taxonomy, thus ensuring a range of activities would be tested. Finally, a distinction should be made between diagnostic models of reading and curriculum models. Many teachers are seeking to develop flexible and sophisticated readers and to provide a range of reading opportunities and experiences. For them a differentiated analysis may provide a guide to planning, assessment and evaluation – although probably not to individual weaknesses.

Diagnosis of Specific Reading Difficulty

Diagnostic phonic tests of the type described in a previous section are not concerned with in-depth diagnosis of causal or underlying difficulties. They claim to do no more than enumerate or map those aspects of phonics and blending that the learner has difficulty with – the 'surface' features of reading difficulty.

For many children this approach, which involves 'finding out what the child cannot do and then teaching accordingly' is probably appropriate. Nevertheless, some remedial reading specialists would argue that there are children for whom this level of diagnosis is not enough. For them phonic difficulty is no more than symptom, due to underlying perceptual or cognitive causes. It is these that must be identified and remedied if the child is to make progress. Tests for assessing such children tend to follow a common pattern in the form of a diagnostic battery of sub-tests, and typical examples will be described below. However, before this approach to diagnosis is considered more fully, some comment should be made on the concept of 'dyslexia'.

Some remedial reading specialists distinguish between learners with 'dyslexia' and those with other kinds of reading difficulties. The term is also sometimes used to describe any reading difficulty due to cognitive and perceptual causes. For those who take this view most of the tests and methods described in this section deal, by definition, with dyslexia. Certainly, the *Aston Index,* to be discussed below, was designed to diagnose dyslexia. Nevertheless, use of the term 'dyslexia' remains controversial, and many teachers and educational psychologists would prefer not to employ it as a label for any of their pupils' or clients' difficulties. Evidence for its existence as a diagnosable syndrome seems to come mainly from clinical experience rather than systematic research. However, it is worth noting that contemporary views of dyslexia emphasize difficulty with writing more than reading and define it as a general difficulty in processing – particularly sequencing – symbolic material (e.g. Miles, 1983; Pavlides, 1979). It may therefore be that tests concerned exclusively with diagnosis of *reading* difficulty – even its specific causes – would not be the best means of diagnosing dyslexia in the above sense. In any case, the discussion which follows will concentrate upon overall strategies for diagnosis and many of the comments in this respect remain valid regardless of the merits of using the term 'dyslexia'.

The Aston Index

The multi-part diagnostic test battery has long provided a standard pattern for individual psychological tests of intelligence and of learning difficulty. In the UK most such tests are normally only supplied to educational psychologists. This ensures that when a child is referred to a psychologist any test-based assessments will not be distorted by prior exposure to the test. The *Aston Index* was the first British test of this pattern which was concerned directly with specific reading difficulty. It was also the first to be made available to teachers as well as psychologists. The Index consists of 17 sub-tests:

General Underlying Ability and Attainment

1. Picture Recognition
2. Vocabulary Scale
3. The *Goodenough Draw-a-man Test**
4. Copying Geometric designs
5. Grapheme-phoneme correspondence
6. Schonell *Graded Word Reading Test*
7. Schonell *Graded Word Spelling Test*.

* This is a widely used procedure for assessing general mental development. The child is instructed to draw a person. The drawing is then rated according to specified guidelines. From this an IQ is derived.

Performance Items

8. Visual discrimination
9. Child's laterality
10. Copying name
11. Free writing
12. Visual sequential memory (pictures)
13. Auditory sequential memory
14. Sound blending
15. Visual sequential memory (symbolic)
16. Sound discrimination
17. Graphomotor test.

The sub-tests are grouped into two levels. Level 1 tests are intended for screening and diagnosis of potential problems. Level 2 tests are intended for assessment of children over 7 years who have failed to make the expected progress. Results are recorded on separate profile charts for General Underlying Ability and Performance Items. The Handbook which accompanies the Index presents examples of these and how they might be interpreted, together with instructions for administering and scoring the tests.

In its content and organization the Index typifies the conventional psychological test battery. Although published in revised form in 1982 the test generally makes use of ideas and material which had been in existence for some time. It incorporates three previously published tests (3, 6 and 7). The others use standard techniques for testing memory and discrimination or involve very simple language activities such as copying one's own name. The difference with convention, as has been noted, is in the test's availability for classroom use. Certainly, it would seem that since original publication in 1976 there has been a gradual trend towards its adoption, particularly by remedial and reading advisory teachers. It seems unlikely that the proposed 'screening' use would be practicable. Screening involves sifting through large numbers of children and the Index would simply take too long for this. However, where a teacher is faced with a child encountering profound difficulty with reading and writing, the Index would provide the most comprehensive conventional diagnostic 'run through' available. However, a later publication from the same source, the *Aston Portfolio,* makes it possible, with checklists, to make similar assessments more conveniently, and is accompanied by much more material for remedial follow-up teaching. It would be wise to compare the two in the light of particular needs and circumstances.

The companion to this book, *A Review of Reading Tests* (Vincent *et al.,* 1983), refers to a number of other tests designed for diagnostic assessment along lines roughly similar to the Aston tests. Of these, the Barking Project Materials (not commercially published at the time of writing) are perhaps the most interesting. These cover many of the areas with which the Index is concerned and include prepared remedial materials. Finally, some reference to Daniels and Diack's *Standard Reading Tests* should be made as this battery of tests, published in a hard-bound book, has been in wide use since 1958 and remains, for many teachers, the 'definitive' diagnostic reading test. However, the depth of diagnosis intended by this test is more akin to that of the phonic tests described in the previous section. Some of the tests do deal with fundamental and specific difficulties, notably in visual discrimination, but the main diagnostic emphasis is upon phonics and word blending skills. In fact, the test is probably used less diagnostically than its authors may have intended. The sub-tests most widely used are those which provide a normative attainment score in units of Reading Age. The same fate seems to have befallen the *Neale Analysis of Reading Ability*. This test consists of a series of increasingly difficult oral reading passages to be used mainly in clinical assessment of reading difficulty. In practice, its main role seems to be as an individual measure of reading attainment.

Checklists

The materials discussed so far are, with few exceptions, commercially published and generally available to teachers. Also, while their main purpose may be diagnostic, they often retain links with standardized testing. Their manuals sometimes refer to reliability and validity studies and a number of 'diagnostic' tests are at least partly standardized. Above all, diagnostic tests involve direct observation of performance on set tasks and, at best, make only peremptory use of a teacher's existing knowledge of a child.

Checklists for reading constitute an alternative approach to assessment in all the above respects. Checklists consist of a list of questions to be answered by the teacher concerning the child's reading. Questions may be extremely specific (e.g. 'Can she or he sound out initial consonants?') or more general (e.g. 'Does she or he read voluntarily or for pleasure?'). Relatively few of them have been commercially published, they are rarely validated or normed and they emphasize teachers' knowledge and observation rather than performance of prescribed test activities.

Of the examples which are accessible in published form Dean and Nichols' *Framework for Reading* is probably the best known. This book presents two sets of checklists dealing with the pre-reading and initial stages and with possible causes of reading difficulty.

Raban (1983) presents three more compact examples. Her Checklist 1 (Reading ability) deals with 16 word-attack strategies. Checklist 2 (Phonic checklist record form) covers 26 items of phonic knowledge grouped in seven stages, while Checklist 3 (Reading record) consists of a form for keeping a cumulative record of individual reading.

These two sets of checklists exemplify some of the immediate 'on paper' advantages of the procedure. A wide range of skills and activities can be covered and the teacher's attention is drawn to questions which it is important to ask about a learner, even if they do happen to be hard to test directly or answer objectively. These will include qualitative features of a child's approach to reading and the use of more or less appropriate strategies which, while observable (e.g. dependence on asking for unknown words) are not conveniently testable. Checklists are thus less obliged to concentrate on the trivial or peripheral in the way direct tests are sometimes accused of doing. Their potential as a basis for individual record keeping is also apparent. In addition, they may have particular value as a structure by which less experienced teachers may monitor reading development and ensure systematic and thorough teaching for all children in a class.

The above merits were termed 'on-paper' as no practically-based evidence seems to be available to support them. There are also obvious disadvantages, of which the time and labour involved in completing them is the most notable. However, in a diagnostic remedial setting this problem may be less acute. Checklists are essentially informal judgemental devices and evidence on such matters as reliability and validity is sparse and not always reassuring. Potton (1983) describes a study showing considerable inaccuracy in a checklist designed to screen for reading failure. The opportunity occasioned by a checklist to ask relevant questions about a child has already been mentioned in this chapter. However, there is a great difference between asking a relevant question and providing a relevant, valid or reliable answer. The way teachers interpret these and the accuracy with which they are answered will be highly variable and, in extreme cases, may not accord at all with the checklist author's intentions. Where published examples are taken simply as patterns or suggestions for developing one's own in-school device, this problem will be lessened. Clift *et al.* (1981), in a general study of school record keeping, found that teachers were most enthusiastic about recording systems which they had helped design as the final point in a curriculum development programme. The researchers found that many systems had little meaning to teachers other than the originators because they made assumptions which had arisen in the course of the development stage. For a checklist to be an effective device it may be necessary for anyone who is to use it to be actively engaged in its creation. This may seem to be 'reinventing the wheel'. Nevertheless, unless the potential users of a checklist have the opportunity to think through its content from first principles for themselves they may not have the insight, understanding and commitment to use it effectively. In fact, systematic use might itself decrease as the teacher became more practised in its application. Where there was less pressure to keep formal records of progress it might begin to serve as an occasional *aide-mémoire*. In effect, the development of a checklist may form a transitional phase in the acquisition of diagnostic skill.

Oral Reading: Miscues Analysis

The appraisal of reading difficulty by analysis of errors made in reading continuous prose is a long-established diagnostic technique. For many years the *Neale Analysis of Reading Ability,* with its graded series of prose passages, has provided a convenient basis for this. Users of the test were directed to use the following categories for classifying errors:

Refusal
Omission
Mispronunciation
Reversal
Substitution.

Experienced teachers would also use the test to make additional observations of children's reading such as use of pictorial clues and self-correction. Nevertheless, in themselves the error categories are of limited diagnostic value.

A further dimension to such conventional error classification has been provided by 'miscues' analysis. This procedure has become the stock in trade of many books and courses on the teaching of reading. However, its importance in relation to reading assessment is considerable and some account of its underlying theory is needed here.

The concept of a reading error as a 'miscue' was originated by Kenneth Goodman (e.g. 1967). He developed a model of reading as a cue-using process which involved a great deal of hypothesizing and inferring in order to comprehend what was being read. Goodman described the process as a 'psycholinguistic guessing game' in which a reader employs a number of sources as cues to the meaning of a test. These would include the reader's knowledge about a range of features of written and spoken language, immediate contextual cues in the reading matter, the reader's pre-existing knowledge about the topic and non-print sources such as illustrations and diagrams. Goodman also argued that conventional phonic decoding – although a mainstay of instruction – was only used, if at all, as a last resort when no other cues were useable.

A feature of the reader's search for meaning is that it is selective – it does not draw on all the resources available. Fluent reading involves the minimum number of cues. Learning to do this inevitably results in some errors, or miscues. An implication of this cue-using model was that misreading might reveal which sources or strategies a reader had not learned to use and whether he or she was overdependent upon or inclined to misapply others. For example, the sentence 'People thought men from Mars had invaded the Earth' will be read by some Junior children as '. . . had *invented* the Earth.' The miscue is close to the spelling and sound of the correct word and is not entirely irrelevant given the preceding context of the passage in which it occurs. It thus shows reasonable but imperfect use of orthographical, phonological and semantic cues. It is also a more 'positive' error than complete refusal or omission. This illustrates an important further aspect of miscues analysis: not all incorrect readings are equally bad. Indeed, some – particularly insertion or omission which make no difference to meaning or grammatical correctness ('. . . *that* men from Mars had invaded Earth') – are symptomatic of fluency rather than reading difficulty.

Goodman's research work has involved the development of a taxonomy (i.e. classification system) of reading miscues. Early versions contained roughly 20 categories of miscues. Each of these is reflected in a question to be asked about the miscue, e.g. 'How much graphic similarity is there between the observed and the expected reading?' 'Does the miscue produce a semantically acceptable text?' The questions and categories they reflect are not mutually exclusive, thus each question may be asked about each miscue. As a result, a qualitative picture of the way a reader operates can be built up.

Miscues analysis originated as a research procedure. An audio recording was made as the research subject read out an unfamiliar text and then verbally recalled as much of its content as possible with limited prompting from the researcher. This latter component provided a measure of comprehension against which the miscues could be compared. Miscues analysis could then be made at leisure.

It would be impracticable to carry out a full miscues analysis for classroom diagnosis. Indeed, some of Goodman's miscue categories are of theoretical rather than practical significance. Yet, the principles of the technique seem to have promise as a teaching aid.

A published 'kit', the *Reading Miscues Inventory*, was produced in 1972. However, this is not readily available in the UK and is, in any case, still relatively elaborate and time-consuming. Arnold (1984) has produced a set of reading materials and a teacher's manual for a simplified version of miscues analysis (*Making Sense of It*) which would be of greater relevance to British teachers. This is based on Arnold's work on the Schools Council Extending Beginning Reading Project, described in *Extending Beginning Reading* (Southgate *et al.*, 1981). The original procedure used in the Schools Council project commences with coding of a recording of the reader's miscues. Each miscue is coded according to the following categories:

Non-response
Hesitation
Repetition
Self-correction
Substitution
Insertion
Omission
Reversal.

In themselves these categories are of limited diagnostic value. However, the next stage requires the evaluation of each miscue by asking four questions about each one. These deal with the graphophonemic, syntactic and semantic levels of language and use of self-correction. A tally is made of the miscues according to contextual and graphic correctness and evidence of positive and negative reading strategies is noted. Detailed case study examples of individual children and their miscues are also presented.

This system was developed primarily for research into miscues and a somewhat simplified version of the original guidelines (also outlined and accompanied by examples in *Listening to Children Reading* (Arnold, 1982)) is employed in *Making Sense of It*. Here miscues are classified in six categories and then rated as either 'Positive' or 'Negative'. Guidelines are given for applying these criteria. For example, in the case of substitutions whether they are positive or negative is established by the extent of what are termed the 'graphophonic', 'grammatical' and 'semantic' appropriateness of the miscues.

The author points out that there is no one correct way of analysing miscues. It is a method that teachers might adapt to suit particular purposes. Goodman himself (1973) suggests a procedure whereby a count is made of miscues which result in acceptable meanings or which are successfully corrected. These, expressed as a percentage of all the miscues made, can be regarded as a measure of the reader's ability to 'keep his focus successfully on meaning'.

To carry out one or two miscues analyses would certainly be a useful exercise for any teacher wishing to gain further insight into the nature of reading. To use such analysis routinely as a diagnostic strategy with individual children would require a more serious study of the theoretical background. It is not a mechanical procedure, but a clinical technique requiring a judicious evaluation of Goodman's model of reading as a search for meaning rather than a simple decoding process. The reference to 'evaluation' is important. Goodman regards learning to read as an extension of the learner's natural capacity to acquire language, and this has controversial implications. For example, Goodman is critical of reliance on phonics, particularly as a basis for diagnostic assessment. While the 'psycholinguistic' approach is not in itself a teaching method, it has challenging implications for method which have to be thought through.

Informal Reading Inventories (IRIs)

Amongst informal and do-it-yourself diagnostic methods the

Informal Reading Inventory (IRI) is the most developed and has been widely discussed in books and journals concerned with reading. It has three main uses:

1. Diagnosis and comparison of oral and silent reading skills, particularly with pupils new to the teacher.

2. Judging the suitability of particular texts and reading material for individual readers.

3. Providing a convenient structure for miscues analysis.

In its simplest form an IRI consists of a text chosen by the teacher and containing no more than 300 words. The child reads this aloud and then verbally answers questions about it. In more developed forms it will include a series of passages taken from texts of increasing difficulty. Each of these is accompanied by a separate word recognition test, containing a selection of unfamiliar words from the passage to which it corresponds. Comprehension questions for each passage will be prepared according to a systematic rationale such as Barrett's Taxonomy, and once the reader has reached a certain level of difficulty some further passages in the series may be given as listening comprehension tests. Fuller details of such an extended approach are given by Strang (1969).

By giving the same IRI to all children in a group a teacher can obtain a reasonable impression of the general range of ability and pick out the weakest readers. Used more interpretively, the IRI may pinpoint noteworthy contrasts between oral and silent reading in some pupils. The IRI may also provide the occasion and opportunity to observe general features of the child's approach to reading: nervousness and lack of confidence; dependence on being told unfamiliar words or absence of any word-getting strategies; self-correction; pointing; perseverance; rate; expression; wild guessing. In effect, the IRI provides a structure for getting to know new 'clients'. It may also be possible to pick up details of phonic knowledge, although this might be done more systematically with phonic tests of the sort discussed in a previous section.

A rather more specialized application is possible in which IRI performance is taken as a guide to the kind of reading a child could carry out with the text from which a test passage has been selected.

The concepts of *Independent, Instructional and Frustration* levels of reading provide the basis for this. At the Independent level a text can be read for a wide variety of purposes, including recreational reading, without any support from the teacher. The customary criterion for this is 99 per cent accuracy in oral reading and correct answers to nine out of ten comprehension questions. The Instructional level is that at which reading needs to be practised and developed for itself. While a text at this level might not be used entirely autonomously by a reader, it would provide an adequate basis for working with teacher support. This is usually set at 95 per cent accuracy and seven out of ten comprehension questions correct. If oral reading accuracy is less than 90 per cent and no more than half the comprehension questions are correct the text is said to be too difficult for any useful purpose – the reader's Frustration level. Some authorities also refer to a *Potential* level, based on the number of correct answers to questions asked after hearing the passage read aloud. This might indicate that a text is one the reader could be expected to move on to subsequently.

The distinction between Independent and Instructional levels of reading is a useful one by which to evaluate a child's current reading matter and judge whether she or he might not be moved on to more demanding or advanced material for some purposes. However, they are no more than rough working categories and must not be treated as real psychological 'states' which have some proven existence. Moreover, the stated numerical criteria should not be taken too literally as researchers continue to look (perhaps in vain) for optimal criteria for these. Finally, it would be naive to treat results of an IRI in isolation from other considerations. When matching books and reader's interest, curiosity and purpose on the part of the intended reader must be set alongside the prognosis from the IRI.

Diagnosis of Comprehension Skills with IRIs

It has been suggested above that IRI comprehension questions should be devised to cover different levels or aspects of comprehension. This will certainly ensure a general spread of comprehension tasks, and it is tempting to try to attach some diagnostic intepretation to these. However, such an exercise is likely to be spurious and misleading. The general difficulty of validating distinct comprehension sub-skills for diagnostic purposes has already been discussed. In the case of the IRI the problem is even more acute. Typically, IRIs employ only a limited number of questions. Apparent 'weakness' on a particular skill could be due to the intrinsic difficulty of the question(s) devised to test that skill as much as to genuine weakness in the comprehension skill tested. The inadequacy of IRIs as diagnostic measures of comprehension is discussed more fully by Schell and Hanna (1981) who refer to a range of obstacles to such use – not the least of these is the difficulty in first preparing questions which teachers will all agree test what they were intended to test.

IRIs for Miscues Analysis

To carry out a miscues analysis it is necessary to have reading matter which is new to the reader and of sufficient difficulty to induce a reasonable number of errors. A competently devised IRI will achieve this. The methods of miscues analysis discussed previously can be readily applied to a tape recording of an IRI. A further method of analysis, developed with IRIs in mind, is described in detail by Pflaum (1979). The author claims a high degree of reliability for the system, which makes separate counts of rates of meaning change, self-correction, self-correction of meaning change, and partial and high use of phonic cues.

The IRI differs from standard miscues analysis procedures in employing formalized comprehension questions rather than more general recall. The latter method may well have greater overall validity as a global check on comprehension. It is not easy to devise entirely flawless verbal comprehension questions which genuinely measure understanding of what has been read. A seemingly reasonable question may be answerable without the reader's actually having understood the reading text. Moreover, it is difficult to devise questions which do not, in themselves, convey the answer to following questions. One solution would be a mixed approach in which unaided verbal recall was attempted before presenting the questions.

Published IRIs

A number of commercially published IRIs is available in the US. Eleven of these are reviewed by Jongsma and Jongsma (1981) and one of these, *Edwards' Reading Test,* is available in the UK. Apart from the convenience of providing ready made material these published examples do not seem to have any advantage over teacher-made versions. None appear to have been validated or standardized in a way which would make them in any way superior to those made by individual teachers. Also, the opportunity to match materials to the immediate context of teaching would be lost.

Cloze Procedure

It is sometimes argued that cloze procedure (outlined in Chapter 1) can be used diagnostically. It would certainly seem possible that errors in responding to cloze tests should give some qualitative indication of the reader's difficulties. It seems that the diagnostic role of cloze procedure is less developed than its use for assessing general comprehension ability or reading attainment. Published versions are certainly of limited diagnostic value. The Bowman test includes 'Syntactic' and 'Semantic' subscores and the NFER *Reading Level Tests* seek to prescribe the readability (i.e. difficulty) level of reading matter to which a child is suited. These are the only examples of published cloze tests which go beyond simple attainment measurement.

There is very little published discussion of diagnosis through cloze procedure. Vincent and Cresswell (1976) tentatively suggest ten points for the diagnostic observation of individual children while attempting cloze tasks. Rye (1982) develops much more fully a scheme for analyzing written responses to cloze. Firstly, errors are classified in four categories, according to syntactic and semantic appropriateness. This gives a finer indication of the severity of a reader's difficulty in comprehension. A child who makes, mainly, errors which are syntactically and semantically appropriate, will have a less severe difficulty than one who makes more errors which are less appropriate by these criteria. The kind of remedial work the first child would require might focus on relatively advanced matters of style. This would not suit a child whose responses were consistently semantically irrelevant.

Rye proposes a second stage of diagnostic analysis which requires detailed appraisal of each error, bearing in mind what the reader may have ignored in making the error and what aspects of the text might explain it. He exemplifies this with notes on individual errors and discusses various forms of remedial action which could follow particular patterns of error. This advice is offered as a set of possibilities, rather than as a standard procedure. The method Rye describes is essentially intuitive and speculative and would have to be undertaken in an exploratory spirit. There is little formal research evidence which would provide guidance on cloze error analysis although Neville and Pugh (1982) report studies which compared cloze answers of good and poor readers on the *GAP Reading Comprehension Test*.

Do Teachers Need Diagnostic Tests?

The materials and procedures reviewed in this chapter have been discussed deliberately in as positive terms as possible. The aim has been to suggest ways in which the teacher in search of an existing structure for diagnostic assessment might best make the most appropriate choice. The larger issue of what place such tests have in the repertoire of professional competence must now be considered. There are certainly experienced and successful teachers who make no use of them or do so only for externally imposed reasons. There is also no direct evidence to show that poor readers who happen to be diagnostically tested make more progress than those who are not. Above all, it cannot be claimed that any diagnostic test contains a key or secret ingredient which gives it special diagnostic powers beyond those which teachers can acquire for themselves.

Nevertheless, not all teachers are experienced. Used thoughtfully, many of the materials and methods reviewed in this chapter could be of considerable value to the teacher faced with poor readers for the first time. One might expect that over time some teachers would become increasingly selective in their use as experience and understanding of the problems of poor readers increased. Some diagnostic materials are particularly suited to this self-training role, notably the *Aston Portfolio* and the *Macmillan Diagnostic Reading Pack* (the manual for this is has the title *Teach Yourself to Diagnose Reading Problems*). There are also more experienced teachers, such as those working in LEA support services, who deal routinely with new referals. The use of a formal test here may be essential both for rapid but systematic initial appraisal and record keeping. There are others who simply happen to find that the use of formal diagnostic tests suits their way of working or the setting in which they teach.

Finally, some of the criticisms of diagnostic tests and methods and reasons given for not using them should be considered.

"There are no poor readers in this school."

If this is the case there is clearly no need for diagnostic assessment. However, many schools will have at least some poor readers. It would be disturbing to learn that this possibility had never been explored – by screening tests, for example – and that therefore the possible value or necessity of diagnostic procedures had simply never been considered.

"We tried 'Test X' and it didn't seem to tell us anything useful."

Sometimes it emerges that 'Test X' was really an attainment test, not a diagnostic one. Did the user really take the time to understand the stated purpose, background and use to the test? Could this mean that no interpretation at all was made because the user did not adequately understand the relevant instructions? Will potentially more suitable alternatives now be tried? Did the user expect 'Test X' to solve problems rather than help explore them? The last question is often the most telling. The expectation that diagnosis will be closely followed by 'cure' (or at least treatment) pervades everyday life. The two thus become closely associated in our minds. Unfortunately, in everyday life we are the *passive* recipients of diagnosis and treatment, be it at the hands of a plumber or surgeon. As diagnosticians, teachers are cast in an unfamiliar *active* role which brings with it the onus of taking the initiative for providing remedies to follow diagnosis. A related criticism is that the test did not tell the teacher anything she or he "did not know already". This may be a reflection of the simplicity of the test used or, again, diagnostic and attainment testing may have been confused. It may also be a favourable reflection of the professional skill of the teacher concerned. One would still wish to know what it was the teacher 'already knew' and whether this knowledge can be articulated and effectively acted upon.

"Diagnostic tests are too time-consuming to use."

This is a common criticism. Some procedures certainly do require the teacher to spend out-of-class time scoring, recording and analysing. Most require relatively long periods of one-to-one testing and this will only be possible where there is special provision for poor readers. Some diagnostic procedures are useable in group form (e.g. Carver's *Word Recognition Test; Swansea Test of Phonic Skills*) and not all individual procedures require a great deal of time (e.g. Assessment Checklist of the *Aston Portfolio*). However, the overall problem of time remains one of resources and priorities within school. If remedial reading is given a relatively low priority then the scope for diagnosis will be greatly limited.

"Testing poor readers creates distress and a sense of failure."

This is a criticism that has more weight in the case of attainment tests designed for assessing a wide range of ability. Some diagnostic tests, particularly at the pre-reading and reading readiness stage, do not require any reading ability whatsoever. Many individual tests commence with the simplest possible material and allow for testing to be discontinued when the child begins to fail. Checklists, of course, largely avoid any direct testing of children.

"Testing results in the misleading labelling of children."

Some critics of testing are rightly concerned that children get labelled 'dyslexic', 'backward' or 'underachiever' by their teachers without good grounds or consideration of what these labels might mean. The greatest danger is that such labels relieve the teacher of responsibility for the child's progress, or lack of it. This criticism can only be answered bluntly. If there is a real danger that diagnostic test results may be treated in this way then it would be better the tests were not used. However, the likelihood of such abuses will be much less where teachers are adequately conversant with the nature of the tests in use in their school and there is some sensitivity and vigilance over the general danger of labelling.

CHAPTER 8

Criterion-Referenced Testing

Educational testing has a strong element of conservatism running through it. Theoretical and technical innovations are slow to percolate into practice and are often regarded with suspicion. Certainly, there is a tendency for the same tests, or types of tests to remain in use year after year. The history of 'criterion-referenced' testing exemplifies this. The idea of criterion-referencing is now 20 years old but its practical impact on the development of reading tests has been slight.

A criterion-referenced test is one which measures *what* a child can do. It deals with the skills or knowledge which have been mastered or the level of competence which has been reached. A parallel is sometimes made between criterion-referenced testing and the Department of Transport driving test.

However, most British published reading tests are *norm*-referenced: they relate a child's performance to a standard or average in the way described in Chapter 5. A norm-referenced reading test score (e.g. an RA or standardized score) simply tells the teacher how much better, or worse, a child's reading is than that of other children. ('Norm-referenced' is really a synonym for 'standardized'.) By contrast, a criterion-referenced score tells the teacher what it is the child can do *as a reader*.

This distinction between norm-referenced tests, which deal with a child's relative status and criterion-referenced tests, which deal with absolute performance, was first made by Glaser (1963). Numbers of books and articles on the theory of criterion-referenced testing were published over the next ten years. These, mainly by American authors, were concerned with programmed learning and behavioural objectives-based teaching, not, primarily, the assessment of reading. Nevertheless, criterion-referenced testing, with its promise of a concrete and specific account of 'what a reader can do' sounds like the ideal solution to many of the testing needs of the reading teacher. Also, the proponents of criterion-referenced testing have found an easy target in pointing out the intrinsic elements of norm-referenced assessment (e.g. Popham 1978, Chapter 4).

In spite of this potential of criterion-referenced testing and the limitations of norm-referenced tests, the would-be user of criterion-referenced reading tests faces a number of problems. At the purely practical level, there is a dearth of published examples to choose from. In 1977 Sumner and Robertson reviewed a selection of published criterion-referenced tests. Eight of these were concerned with language but only one – Daniels and Diack's *Standard Reading Tests* – could be regarded as widely used. (This test was also published in 1958, before the concept of criterion-referenced tests had been formalized or discussed in published sources.) In *A Review of Reading Tests,* criterion-referenced tests are sparsely represented. Although the standard American review of published tests, the *Eighth Mental Measurements Yearbook* (Buros, 1978), lists over 30 criterion-referenced tests, only two of these are available in the UK. Thus, for British teachers, criterion-referenced assessment remains more a concept than a reality.

Secondly, there is a major problem of defining precisely what is meant by a criterion-referenced test, even though there may be agreement about the general principles involved. Some authors also prefer to use terms such as content-referenced test, domain-referenced test or mastery testing (and more wryly, cloud-referenced and pseudo-referenced tests) to distinguish between different applications of the principle.

Nitko (1980) in an article entitled 'Distinguishing the Many Varieties of Criterion-Referenced Tests', provides an excellent guide through the confusion. He argues that criterion-referenced tests can be classified according to the way they relate to the 'domain of behaviour' they measure. He suggests four main types of domains:

Well-defined and ordered domains	Ill-defined domains
Well-defined but unordered domains	Undefined domains.

A domain is said to be well defined when it is clear 'which categories of performances (or which kind of task) should and should not be considered as potential test items'. In reading terms, this amounts to a clear specification of what it is that the reader is required to do. A test must relate to a clearly defined domain to be regarded as a valid criterion-referenced test.

Well-defined and Ordered Domains (scales)

If it is possible to specify a sequence or hierarchy of performance or learning, the domain is said to be ordered in addition to being well-defined. Nitko speaks of tests which measure such ordered domains as criterion-referenced achievement 'scales'. There is a number of ways in which such scales can be formed and Nitko cites examples of handwriting scales in which writing samples are rated in relation to standard specimens, and spelling scales, based on graded lists. Scales based on Piaget's developmental stages provide further examples.

Well-defined but Unordered Domains (tests)

It is not always possible to specify a particular sequence or continuum for the material or skills to be learned, even though one can be explicit about what the skills are. Here, Nitko speaks of 'tests' rather than 'scales' and again gives categories and examples. Of particular importance are tests based on 'verbal statements of stimuli and responses'. Typically, there are tests devised to measure a specific behavioural objective. Items are produced to conform to a very clear specification of form and content. Popham's IOX tests, (see Sumner and Robertson (1977) and Vincent and Cresswell (1976) for a description of a reading test in this series) exemplify this approach. Unordered domains may also be used as a basis for 'diagnostic categories'. These include tests for some forms of readiness for learning (possibly reading readiness), and for 'missing-component behaviour' which might include many of the diagnostic tests mentioned in Chapter 7. Finally, Nitko notes there are published norm-referenced tests which have taken on 'a criterion-referenced hue'. His examples include some American reading tests.

Ill-defined and Undefined Domains

Nitko refers to the existence of tests which their developers claim to be criterion-referenced on the basis of poorly specified or ambiguous domains. These he discounts as criterion-referenced tests together with those where the domain is defined only in terms of the particular items on the test. He also dismisses tests which adopt a 'cutoff score' which is not directly related to 'a domain of instructionally relevant performances'. Such tests may provide some notional yardstick – for example the NFER *English Proficiency Tests* – but they do not qualify as criterion-referenced tests unless the cutoff score relates to a well-defined domain.

How well does reading lend itself to criterion-referencing in terms of 'well-defined domains'? The answer, perhaps, depends upon which side of the Atlantic one is teaching. There are plenty of highly developed American criterion-referenced tests of reading. Few of these 'travel well', as they go in for a degree of detail and complexity which would seem excessive, if not ludicrous, to British teachers (see, for example, STARS in *A Review of Reading Tests*).

There are certainly some areas of reading which constitute well-defined domains. In phonics, for example, it is possible to be very precise about the content and objectives of teaching. McLeod's *Domain Test of Phonic Skills* is a clear example of a phonic criterion-referenced 'test' in Nitko's sense. Carver's *Word Recognition Test* goes some way to constituting a 'scale' as the author suggests that there is a sequence of phonic development upon which the test is based – albeit a loose and general one. Downing's test for the acquisition of concepts about written language for reading readiness, *LARR*, suggests another well-defined, but unordered, domain. Similarly, the NFER *Reading Level Tests* show how readability (the measured difficulty of a book or passage) might in a sense constitute an ordered domain.

Reading comprehension has proved less easy to map or analyse convincingly as a domain, as Chapter 7 has already remarked.

Unless a way can be found to differentiate various aspects of comprehension it is meaningless to think in terms of criterion-referenced testing.

The practical problems of producing a satisfactory account of domains in reading has clearly dogged the producers of published criterion-referenced tests. Reviewers of many of the entries in the *Eighth Mental Measurements Yearbook* find the domains and associated objectives inadequately defined.

One alternative approach so far seemingly untried would be to produce a 'task analysis', carried out by teachers who sought to identify the ways they require children to *use* reading in the classroom. Having done this, it might make sense to devise tests which ascertain how far children have, in practice, learned to apply reading effectively in the ways identified.

A final major problem concerns the production of criterion-referenced tests of quality. It has already been noted that criterion-referenced assessment is a largely American phenomenon and that few tests of US origin are sold in the UK. This is just as well. The critical tone of reviews in Buros has already been mentioned. While a considerable academic and technical literature exists on how to produce good criterion-referenced tests, few test producers have managed to put this theory into practice. Hambleton and Eignor (1978) have published some interesting 'Guidelines for Evaluating Criterion Referenced Tests and Test Manuals' covering ten aspects of criterion-referenced tests:

A   Objectives
B   Test Items
C   Administration
D   Test Layout
E   Reliability
F   Cut-off Scores
G   Validity
H   Norms
I   Reporting Test Score Information
J   Test Score Interpretation.

They evaluated 11 published tests, including six reading tests, against specific criteria in each of these categories. While they found few problems regarding C, D and H there were other important respects in which tests were unacceptable.

In all, Hambleton and Eignor proposed over 39 questions to be asked about criterion-referenced tests. Whilst not all of these are entirely relevant to testing in British schools, some are worth consideration here, as they highlight some of the main problems in producing criterion-referenced tests.

A8 '*Does the set of objectives measured by the test serve as a representative set from some content domain of interest?*' (All the tests met this criterion – 'with reservations'.)

We have noted that this is a key problem for assessing reading. It is of course possible arbitrarily to define a domain and then elaborate upon the objectives for teaching and testing in this 'domain'. For the reading teacher the problem of defining a valid or worthwhile domain remains.

B1 '*Is the item review process described?*'
B2 '*Are the test items valid indicators of the objectives they were developed to measure?*'

In developing criterion-referenced tests the validation of items by *a priori* judging, rating and classification is of major importance. This involves subject area specialists in a variety of procedures to judge whether an item is congruent with the specification of what it is to measure. In the case of reading this raises the question of who is, and who is not, a specialist or 'expert'.

E1 *Is the type of reliability information offered in the test manual appropriate for the intended use (or uses) of the scores?*

Few of the tests evaluated by Hambleton and Eignor met this criterion. There is an extensive literature on ways by which the reliability of criterion-referenced tests might be established. It is agreed that the conventional methods discussed in Chapter 4 are not entirely appropriate and a variety of alternatives has been suggested. (Popham (1978) discusses some of them in general, non-technical terms.) However, this is clearly a point on which any future tests will require particular scrutiny.

F3   Was evidence for the validity of the chosen cut-off score (or cut-off scores) offered?

The concept of a cut-off score is fundamental to a criterion-referenced test, which by definition divides those who have not mastered a learning objective from those who have. Few of the tests evaluated met this requirement, however. The problem is one of establishing the 'right' or optimal cut-off point. Ideally, this requires an experimental study of the relationship between test scores and some appropriate external criterion measure. This would often be hard to apply to reading tests. Some published tests measure a series of skills and objectives by single items. If the child fails an item it is assumed the skill has not been learned. This evades the problem of a cut-off score, but can raise more serious problems of reliability.

The above five questions, *at least,* should be asked in appraising any new criterion-referenced test of reading.

As an ideal or principle criterion-referenced assessment has much to offer the teacher of reading. The development of criterion-referenced testing has been a largely American phenomenon. Its application, notably in objectives-based teaching, may not be entirely appropriate in British schools.

The concept of a domain which provides the objectives for teaching and assessment is central to criterion-referenced testing, but domains in reading, particularly as comprehension, are hard to define. Here, perhaps, there is an as yet unanswered challenge to the teacher of reading to articulate what it is the learner must be taught to do as a reader.

So far, few published criterion-referenced tests are available to British teachers. Many of those produced outside the UK are dubious examples and strict criteria such as those proposed by Hambleton and Eignor need to be applied to future versions.

CHAPTER 9

Beyond Reading Ability

There are many important aspects of reading which cannot be 'tested'. There are also many aspects of written and spoken language for which testing is of dubious relevance or is rarely carried out because of the dearth of appropriate tests or techniques. To discuss these is to highlight the limitations to testing methods in general. At the same time, such discussion will raise the question of whether teachers should be prepared to make much fuller use of non-test media for assessment.

Reading Attitudes, Values and Interests

Tests of reading deal exclusively with reading as a cognitive ability. They measure the reader's capacity to perform tasks of varying difficulty. They can do this directly, by testing overt oral reading behaviours, or indirectly, by examining how well a reader carries out tasks requiring silent reading. In effect, they deal with reading as a functional skill which is characteristically used upon non-fictional texts.

However, teachers of reading are equally concerned with reading as a recreational and imaginative experience which engages the reader's response at an emotional or 'affective' level as well as cognitively. This may be seen simply as a matter of seeking to develop enjoyment of books for its own sake. More complex analyses are possible which take pleasure and enjoyment as the starting point for the eventual development of literary sensibility and the humanizing effects of literature. In either case, we seem to be in the realms of the untestable.

This is not to say that there are no formal ways in which teachers can gather information. For example, it is a fairly simple business to keep a record of the number and titles of books borrowed or bought by children. Activity of this sort is a necessary (but not sufficient) condition for achievement of the values noted above. It is also possible to obtain more specific information about the quality of such reading. The *Ingham Reading Record Form* (Ingham 1983) provides an interesting published example of how this can be done. The Record consists of a single sheet containing ten simple questions to be answered when the reader first chooses the book or has stopped reading it. Over time, these allow a cumulative picture of a reader's development to be formed.

Worthwhile information can be obtained on a more general scale, also. It can be argued that if it is important for a school to carry out annual surveys of reading performance it could be equally important to find out routinely about the development of attitudes, habits and interests. Data of this sort could be just as informative a guide to teaching and curriculum planning as standardized test results. It may also be a basis for evaluating certain changes or innovations in practice; for example, introduction of book clubs or visits to school by children's authors. Admittedly, this is less frequently done than standardized testing. The range of ready-made materials for such undertakings is limited and they require certain additional expertise. Nevertheless, many teachers on advanced in-service courses are introduced to the methods of survey and attitude research. Their use is not beyond the scope of a sufficiently committed teacher.

The term 'attitude' needs further comment. Teachers often say that they are just as concerned to develop 'good attitudes' to reading as with increasing reading skill. However, individuals might not fully agree as to what constituted a 'good' attitude. At the most elementary level, good or hoped-for attitudes might be defined by certain responses to the questions the teacher has chosen to ask, either by pencil-and-paper questionnaires or individual interviewing. These may deal with more or less factual matters ('How many books have you read?' 'Where do you usually read them?') or areas of feeling and opinion ('Do you enjoy reading?' 'Do you like comics?'). Interpretation of results will be on a question-by-question basis. This will enable the teacher to construct an overall impression of how far intended aims are being achieved.

The teacher in the above example could not claim to be measuring attitudes although he or she might reasonably claim to be assessing them in the light of the data obtained. However, attitude measurement is widely undertaken in social research and has occasionally been attempted in reading research – notably by the APU.

Attitude measurement requires an instrument which can *quantify* the strength or extent to which different individuals hold the same attitude. It also differs from the above example in being confined to the individual's feelings, beliefs and orientation towards a subject. It stops short of observing overt behaviours. Strictly speaking, a reader could have a strong positive attitude towards books and reading but rarely do any reading. The criteria for developing attitude measures are also more stringent than those for devising questionnaires or interviews. Although there is no 'right answer' to an attitude item, the procedures for developing attitude measures, or *scales,* are otherwise very similar to those for standardized tests described in Chapters 3 and 4.

There are diverse techniques and formats for preparing attitude scale items. Given that attitudinal assessment in reading is rarely carried out, and no commercially published scales are available in the UK, it would be a somewhat arid task to review these in detail. Pumphrey and Dixon (1970) discuss some scales that have been used by reading researchers and the APU's Language Monitoring reports present details of instruments – including the actual items – used for national surveys of 11 and 15-year-olds.

Although the APU is not officially concerned with producing instruments for use by teachers, its *Language Performance in Schools* reports are probably the most accessible source of examples and data which, with some adaptation or elaboration, might be capitalized upon for assessing attitudes in individual classrooms. This topic is developed further in Chapter 10.

Before leaving non-cognitive aspects of reading, some mention should be made of 'self-concept'. The essence of self-concept theory is that the way in which individuals perceive themselves affects the way they function. More specifically, the person someone believes him or herself to be is the person he or she tends to become or continues to be. Children who have an image of themselves as poor readers will thus read poorly – regardless of their underlying potential to become proficient readers. In appraising a child's reading problem it can be useful to know how far this is accompanied by a negative image of self as a reader. Educational researchers have made considerable use of self–rating scales to measure the extent to which pupils hold positive or negative self-images. Various examples dealing with self-image in general educational contexts are to be found in Cohen (1976). These suggest ways in which a teacher could produce a reading-specific example for classroom use. However, serious consideration should be given to the alternative of exploring self-concept by individual interviews. Where time allows this would probably be a more informative and dependable method.

Writing Ability

Reading is only half of literacy, and there have been various attempts to produce tests dealing with the other half – writing ability. The problems of producing standardized tests for writing are even more formidable than those associated with reading. The notion of 'testing' writing via standardized instruments composed of discrete writing items is, ultimately, to overlook that writing is a communication skill. This has not deterred test constructors from developing standardized tests, of which the NFER *English Progress Series* and the *Bristol Achievement Tests, English Language* (Brimer 1969) are major examples. Although entitled 'English' tests these concentrate upon the mechanical aspects of basic literacy and bear little relation to a well-balanced English curriculum.

As tests of reading they break no new ground beyond that discussed in Chapter 1. As tests of writing they concentrate very largely upon grammatical correctness and conventions of punctuation, style, usage and spelling. For the sake of convenience and objectivity the amount of original writing required by such tests is kept to a minimum. In summary, these tests deal with circumstantial evidence about writing ability; at best they include editorial and correcting activities which are subsidiary or subsequent to writing itself. It might be argued in their favour that their results tend to agree with scores based on direct assessment of written work and that they have the advantage of expressing literacy in normative terms. Against this must be set the dangers of perpetuating in test form a misleading and inaccurate model of what literacy is.

Standardized measurement methods thus have only a limited role in the assessment of writing. There is no substitute for methods which require direct judgement of what a writer has written. This raises a completely new set of major topics which, to be introduced adequately, would require a further book in their own right. These include the relative merits of impression marking versus specific 'analytic' guidelines or formalized linguistic criteria, the merits of multiple marking, the nature of the writing tasks to be employed and the possibility of establishing norms or standard examples against which a piece of writing can be appraised.

A useful further discussion of these problems is given in the first APU Language Monitoring report (APU 1981). Some practical first steps in writing assessment are suggested in Stibbs (1979) while more sophisticated models for evaluating written language are to be found in Wilkinson *et al.* (1980). Amongst published test materials the *Hunter-Grundin Literacy Profiles*, the NFER *English Proficiency Tests* and NFER *Transitional Assessment Modules* in English involve assessment of continuous writing tasks.

Oral Ability

Concern is sometimes expressed that reading and writing are emphasized at the expense of oracy – communication in spoken language. It is also argued that a balanced assessment of language should give equal weight to oracy and literacy. As in the case of writing, there have been attempts to lure spoken language into the confines of standardized testing. Standardized tests of 'listening ability', for example, have long been available in the US. However, these adopt an extremely naive model of oral language in which the test material consists of verbally-presented texts as a basis for comprehension and recall tasks. These really present written language in spoken form. They appear to place a high premium upon memory and concentration and provide very little assessment of the listener's ability to process real spoken language. Amongst published tests only the *Schools Council Oracy Project Listening Comprehension Tests* (Wilkinson *et al.*, 1974) really tackle this problem. This much-underrated battery of three tests for top Juniors, middle Secondary pupils and young adults deals with some of the subtler features of spoken language such as register, intonation and implied relationships between speakers. They do not appear to be widely used and remain much ahead of their time.

Formal assessment of a child's spoken language raises both practical and theoretical problems. Considerable demands are made upon time and resources in obtaining and assessing samples of pupils' spoken language. Even if this major problem were overcome, the question of *context* would remain. A person who can communicate effectively in one situation may not necessarily be able to do so in another. This will be determined by a complex set of factors of which knowledge of the linguistic conventions that obtain in the situation could be but one. Perhaps the best that a teacher could expect to achieve would be an impression of a child's spoken competence based on guidelines such as those presented in Tough (1976).

Standardized and formalized testing has, by contrast, played a substantial role in the sphere of diagnostic assessment of language difficulty. This field is very clearly reviewed by Muller *et al.* (1981) who evaluate the use of a number of published diagnostic tests designed for appraisal of speech impairment. Although written principally for speech therapists, this text would be of value to remedial teachers wishing to extend their knowledge of assessment in the specialist area of spoken language difficulty.

CHAPTER 10

Language Monitoring: the Assessment of Performance Unit

Many passing references have already been made to the work of the Assessment of Performance Unit (APU). No introduction to the testing of reading would be complete without mention of the APU, and some further comments will be made here. The APU is a department within the DES which was set up in 1974 with a number of national responsibilities for educational assessment. In practice this has involved the commissioning of test development projects for use in national monitoring surveys in a number of curriculum areas, including language.

The development of tests for language has been the responsibility of a team of researchers at the National Foundation for Educational Research (NFER). This team has produced tests and assessment techniques for reading and writing skills of pupils of 11 and 15 years and at the time of writing these are being used in a five-year programme of annual surveys in England and Wales and a comparable exercise is being carried out in Northern Ireland. In addition, the NFER team is engaged upon developing tehniques for assessing oral ability.

The general work of the APU has been described and evaluated by a number of commentators. The fullest of these is by Gipps and Goldstein (1983) while Satterly (1981) has a useful introductory chapter which also explains some of the technical issues associated with the APU. The APU itself distributes leaflets and newsletters about its work and findings and so far four reports of language surveys – *Language Performance in Schools* – have been published (APU 1981, 1982a, 1982b, 1983).

An undertaking to monitor educational attainment on a national scale is, inevitably, controversial, and critical accounts can be found in Lawton (1980) and Holt (1981). The APU language monitoring in particular is criticized at length by Rosen (1982). Interestingly, the ETSP found that teachers themselves regarded the APU with much less suspicion than the academic critics. Whether this indicates professional naivity or refusal to succumb to hysteria could be debated at length. Yet, whatever the grounds for misgivings, the fact that the APU has been responsible for some noteworthy developments in language testing cannot be ignored. These should provoke thought and re-appraisal about teaching and assessment in schools. For example, the APU has sought to devise better means of assessing oral ability and this work – in progress at the time of writing – has at least enlivened professional debate on the subject (e.g. Barnes 1980). The model of speaking ability adopted by the APU would appear to be highly promising. Some conventional methods of assessing and formally examining oral ability focus upon 'correctness' of speech, enunciation and voice production, or treat 'listening' as a passive act, involving comprehension of aurally-presented texts. By contrast, the APU speaking tests are concerned with overall effectiveness of communication in settings which involve *interaction* between speaker and listener and include solution of problems and conveying instructions.

In assessment of writing the APU has largely rejected the idea of discrete test items, basing assessment primarily upon children's continuous writing. The selection of activities and purposes for writing has also been notably broad and diverse. For example, in the 1980 Primary survey (APU 1982b) twelve different writing tasks were employed. One of these was a short task to be attempted by all children after which each child attempted one of ten different tasks, followed by a 'text-based' exercise, such as editing or annotation. Finally, some brief questions about the pupil's attitudes to writing were presented. The APU's work on writing assessment has occasioned also some useful explorations into the objectivity of teachers' judgements of children's writing ability.

The APU approach to reading assessment includes two features of particular importance. The most evident of these is the way testing is based on comprehension of self-contained free-standing texts which deal with topics over a number of pages. In effect, the test involves working with books in a way not dissimilar to that required in everyday school work. It is also worth noting, in passing, that any temptation to categorize items according to misleading categories of sub-skills was resisted. Test items were written to reflect plausible purposes for reading – not inferred psychological processes. While the full tests themselves are not available for use by schools they provide a format worth emulating in commercially published tests.

Secondly, the APU testing programme has included the assessment of attitudes, interests and habits much more fully than any commercially published materials have done. It has already been noted (Chapter 9) that there is a shortage of commercially available materials for assessing attitudinal facets of reading. Yet here the APU materials could be of direct help. Two main techniques were developed to assess attitudes to reading amongst 11 and 15-year-olds. Firstly, a series of sentence stems consisting of open-ended statements about various aspects of reading (e.g. 'I need to be able to read because . . .') were devised. Pupils complete each sentence in a way which reflects their feelings about the aspect of reading referred to in the stem. Secondly, a number of attitude scales, consisting of statements about reading (e.g. 'Reading stories helps me relax') has been developed. The pupil indicates strength and direction of agreement to these items on a five-point scale (YES, yes, not sure, no, NO).

The complete sets of both types of items are presented in the APU language monitoring reports with much accompanying normative data for each item. For example, in the 1980 Primary survey (APU 1982b) the responses of a national sample of 500 children to the item 'I get involved in what I'm reading' is tabulated as follows:

yes	62.7%
not sure	19.9%
no	12.6%

The results are also given separately for boys and girls.

Responses to open-ended items are classified according to a category system devised by the APU/NFER team. This system is not fully disclosed in the reports, but some of the categories employed are revealed in the course of the discussion. For example, the report of the 1980 survey (APU 1982b) reveals that responses to the stem 'I need to be able to read because . . .' were grouped as follows:

a.	need to cope with everyday life	20%
b.	means of developing knowledge	15%
c.	need to read for enjoyment	13%
d.	filling spare time	5%
e.	avoidance of social embarrassment	2%
f.	essential for schoolwork	31%
g.	for future employment	29%

There are a number of ways the APU reports might serve as a resource for teachers wishing to evaluate reading attitudes. The loosest and most general use would be to take the material in the reports as a guide to the sorts of questions teachers might prepare for their own pupils.

Such an approach probably underuses the wealth of data in the APU's reports. A more specific use might be to select actual stems or statements and present them to a class or large group. An at least rough comparison might then be made of the percentage of class responses in positive and negative categories with those reported for national samples by the APU. The teacher using this approach would have to bear in mind that the APU materials and their results refer to readers of 11 or 15 years. Caution would be needed in using materials with other age groups. Also, it would be inadvisable to treat the proportions of positive and negative responses to particular items within any one school or class as exact reflections of the division of opinions or attitudes in the group. They will certainly be less reliable than those reported by the APU for national samples.

A further elaboration would be to use sets of the APU yes/no response statements as scales. This would allow the teacher not only to compare groups of children against norms for particular items, but also to obtain individual measures of children's attitudes by totalling responses over a set of items. It is evident from the language monitoring reports that the yes/no statements can be grouped into specific sub-sets or sub-scales which deal with particular facets of reading attitude. Unfortunately the research and development work associated with this is not reported in sufficient detail and there are somewhat confusing variations in the way scales are labelled. However, from the secondary survey reports it would seem that initially statements made by pupils in response to open-ended pilot materials were selected and grouped under the following headings:

Independent reading and reading aloud
Content and type of reading material
Motives for reading
Reluctant or negative attitudes towards reading
School activities associated with reading.

As a result of both pilot trials and use of items in main surveys, certain statistical groupings of items were identified. These appear to be similar to the initial groupings and the report of the 1980 Secondary survey (APU 1983) presents the following groupings of itsm into scales:

Pleasure in independent, extended reading (14 items)
Reluctance towards extended reading (15 items)
Reading for self-improvement (8 items)
Preference for factual reading (10 items)
Attitudes towards reading aloud (8 items)
Attitudes to school activities associated with reading (8 items).

The items which comprise each scale are identified, average scale scores for boys and girls are presented graphically, and adequate reliability values are reported for each scale.

Similar scales are derived from the Primary level materials (APU 1982b):

Pleasure in independent, extended reading (8 items)
Preference for reading as a leisure activity (6 items)
Preference for factual reading (7 items)
Reluctance towards extended reading (10 items)
Preference for reading aloud rather than to self (7 items)
Dislike of reading aloud (7 items)
Reading for self-improvement (7 items).

Again graphical indications of average response levels on each scale are provided and the items associated with each scale are listed.

In the absence of fully-developed published materials these scales might be employed, albeit with caution, by class teachers who are willing to read the relevant reports with sufficient care. However, it cannot be stressed too strongly that such scales should not be treated as measures of an individual reader's performance or worth. In the first place, the APU scales are not tests of achievement. Their correlations with performance on the APU tests, although statistically significant, are consistently low. This means that while there may be some very general underlying association between attitude and attainment the two must be treated as independent rather than interchangeable. Responses to attitude statements can be distorted by the pupil's perception of what sort of responses a teacher is looking for and, more profoundly, it can be argued that attitude is too ephemeral or transient a concept to be safely used in assessing or recording individual educational progress. Thus, if the APU scales are to be 'borrowed' or adapted for classroom use, certain criteria should therefore be observed. All responses should remain anonymous, results for individual items should be treated as no more than suggestive of differences with national norms, and it should be appreciated that the results may reflect upon the resources available for reading or the methods and efforts of the teacher, but they cannot fairly reflect upon the 'efforts' of the learner.

The APU has thus been the source of some positive and interesting developments and there is no question but that the APU model of language assessment – whatever its shortcomings – is appealing in its breadth. The hope of some of its advocates that it could result in 'benign backwash' on the language curriculum in some schools is not an unworthy one. The APU has also made some valuable contributions to research into testing. The finding that exposure to particular types of language activity (for example, cloze procedure) led to no positive superiority in tests of those activities (Tuson and Willmott 1983) is a salutory one.

There have been disappointments. The APU has not managed to cast light on allegations of illiteracy amongst school leavers. Also, the practical impact of the APU on the everyday work of reading teachers has been slight. This may be partly intentional.

The APU was not planned with the intention of directly intervening in individual schools or as a direct means of influencing school curricula. Schools are selected entirely randomly, as are the children to be tested. Results for individual children and schools remain strictly confidential as does the content of the majority of the tests used. The results of APU language monitoring surveys – although usually published – are presented at length in dry DES reports which make dull reading. This has been an obstacle to wider discussion, although accessible summary reports are also distributed. However, there has recently been a distinct development in APU reporting policy designed to ensure wider dissemination of its findings. The full reports of the annual surveys will continue to be written and circulated using less expensive reprographic methods, but greater use will be made of newsletters, short reports and occasional papers intended for a wider audience both within and beyond the teaching profession. The following short reports for teachers are likely to be available by the end of 1984: *The Framework for the Assessment of Language,* Tom Gorman; *The Assessment of Writing – Pupils Aged 11 and 15,* Janet White; *Speaking and Listening: an introduction to the surveys of pupil performance at primary level,* Margaret MacLure and Mary Hargreaves. In addition, an overview report summing up the findings over the first five year cycle of annual surveys will be produced.

CHAPTER 11

Parents; Micros; Publishers

Parents

There are three topics which require some mention in an introductory text on the testing of reading but which do not require or lend themselves to sustained treatment. These are the communication of test results to parents, the implications of microcomputers for the testing of reading and the role of commercial publishers. This chapter presents some brief introductory comments on these miscellaneous issues.

The question of whether and how test results can be communicated to parents is the one of the three which is probably of the most immediate professional concern. There is a respectable, but by no means universal, body of opinion that parents have an absolute right to know results of any tests administered to their children. Under certain circumstances this right is supported officially. It has already been noted (Chapter 6) that disclosure of test results to parents may be adopted as LEA policy. Also, if information about reading attainment is to be included in a Statement of Special Educational Needs in accordance with the 1981 Education Act it might possibly take the form of test results. However, the referral of children to specialist reading centres does not, itself, require a Statement and at the time of writing it is not clear how far reading tests might generally feature in the preparation of Statements. Gulliford (1983) in a review of school-based assessment procedures in the context of the 1981 Act appears to see some role for formal testing, alongside professional judgement. However, previous chapters have, by implication, emphasized the role of tests in making decisions about teaching, rather than decisions about children. This deserves to be reiterated more strongly here. Many reading tests are adequate for making tentative and reversible decisions about how one will teach a child – their faults notwithstanding. None are sufficiently authoritative to make decisions which could have far-reaching consequences for children.

The communication of more or less specialized or technical information to a lay client is not easy. As we have seen, standardized reading testing does have a technical dimension. Indeed, it is questionable whether all teachers who use reading tests are, themselves, conversant with technical information of the sort outlined in Chapters 3 and 4. The problem is to make test results meaningful in lay terms without delivering a complete lecture along these lines to every parent who visits a school or whose child has been assessed. It is of course possible to avoid direct reference to scales or scores and couch the information in generalized terms to the effect that the child is 'average', 'below average' or 'above average' at reading. In the case of assessing special needs this might be seen by some as contrary to the principles of partnership and openness referred to in Circular 1/83. A more ethical alternative might be to make use of simplified standardized score scales such as 'stanines' (see Chapter 5) which place readers into one of nine or ten major groups. These are not often used in British schools but do provide general 'bands' that might be more easily understood – and are less misleadingly exact – than a standardized score which can take any value between 60 and 140.

The need to communicate with parents provides further grounds for abandoning the Reading Age scale. To tell parents that their child 'has a reading age of X years' is intrinsically misleading. What the teacher really means is that *when the child was tested on such and such a date (perhaps some time ago) she or he obtained a particular raw score which happens to correspond with the raw score reached by only half of the children with a chronological age of X.* It is quite possible that by the time teacher and parent meet the child's reading age will have increased simply because children's reading ages tend to increase as they get older! To describe a child's ability in terms of age-adjusted standardized scores is less misleading. A standardized score, even if it was obtained on a test given weeks previously, remains a plausible estimate of a child's current position in relation to the average. It would be even better to say that the parent can be 95 per cent certain that the child's score is between value A and value B, employing the standard error as described in Chapter 4.

Head teachers sometimes refer to a child's reading age as a means of impressing a point upon a parent. A dramatic discrepancy between chronological and reading ages may be used to alter unrealistic parental expectations or perceptions. In most such situations the information will be used to support claims which are all too evident to the child's teacher. Reading age may thus be employed as a 'blunt instrument'. It would be presumptuous to condemn this out of hand without consideration of particular circumstances. The reference to discrepancy itself may be the most tenable part of the argument as it is reasonable to expect this will remain stable over time. However, it would be sheer deception to inflate the discrepancy by subtracting reading age *at time of testing* from *current* chronological age.

Computerized Testing?

At the time of writing the impact of microcomputers on the teaching of reading in general has been fairly modest. More significant advances are probably being made currently in the field of word-processing and children's writing. Nevertheless, it would be reasonable to anticipate substantial developments in the reading field. There are certainly two ways in which the increasing use of microcomputers in schools might soon affect the testing of reading. Firstly, testing might be carried out by microcomputer, so that screen and keyboard 'replace' paper and pencil methods of silent testing. Secondly, microcomputers could be used in a managerial role to analyse and store test results and provide fuller analysis of individual and group performance than is practical for teachers to carry out by hand. Of these two possibilities, the latter would seem to be the most likely to be realized in the short term.

It would be a fairly simple task to adapt most pencil-and-paper tests to a screen and keyboard format on the types of micro-computer generally used in British schools. Items or text could be displayed on the screen and responses, either multiple-choice selections or written answers, could be entered via a keyboard. At least one cloze procedure test has been produced in this form (*Wordamatics 1*, Microcomputer Support, ILEA Educational Computing Centre). There would be the added advantages of automatic marking and recording of results. It is also possible to 'tailor' testing individually so that more or less demanding items are selected according to the individual's performance on preceding items. However, most group tests are used to assess reading attainment in class or year groups and results are usually required promptly. This requires sufficient keyboards and screens to enable simultaneous testing of reasonable numbers. At the time of writing few – if any – schools are so lavishly equipped. Also, in adapting existing tests, it would be necessary to establish that the new medium of test administration could be regarded as interchangeable with the conventional printed form. This may not be a problem where short discrete items are involved but difficulties could arise where there is insufficient room to display a complete text on the screen. Here completely different screen and text handling skills may come into play.

Of more immediate interest is the possibility of using microcomputers to store and analyse test results. At present many schools probably under-analyse the results of internal testing programmes. Results tend to be recorded on class or year lists and then forgotten about. This is partly because the necessary statistical expertise has been lacking but the sheer amount of clerical work and hand-computation has probably been the greater obstacle.

The production of annual and cumulative summary statistics, production of group and individual profiles and long-term evaluation of trends and progress seem obvious areas where much more use could be made of computers. It is reasonable to suppose that publishers with a specialist interest in educational testing will give increasing attention to the commissioning and production of programme packages for this purpose.

There are more radical implications of microcomputing and information technology for literacy which should be considered. For example, the reading, accessing and sifting of text stored electronically may involve certain reading skills different in kind from those required to deal with conventional printed texts. Some of these may be relatively trivial, such as processing print presented on screen rather than paper. Others may be more profound, such as the skills and knowledge needed to make effective use of a large computerized data-base. There are also implications for the use of written language, for example, as an essential component in dialogue with a computer. Increased popular use of word-processing also holds both problems and potentials for teaching and assessment. However, it would be precipitous to anticipate the needs for assessment and diagnosis these will bring before much more is realized about the changes they will effect in the way children are required to use and process language.

Educational Test Publishers

This final matter – the role of publishers in the testing of reading – may not at first seem an essential subject for inclusion in an introductory guide to reading tests. In fact, the influence of educational publishers on school curricula in general is easily overlooked. In the case of reading the kinds of tests available from commercial sources have largely determined the quality of assessment in schools. It is easy to blame educational publishers for the inadequacy of much testing which is carried out – "Why don't they produce better tests?" This overlooks the two-way nature of the relationship between publishers and teachers. Tests are a commercial commodity like any other published educational material. The type of test published is partly governed by considerations of profitability and demand. Publishers thus tend to publish the sorts of tests they think teachers will buy. The conservatism of the reading test market has been mentioned in an earlier chapter. Teachers are reluctant to adopt new tests or procedures and slow to abandon long-established ones. Certain reading tests have sold steadily over many years (The *Standard Reading Tests,* first published in 1958, entered a 13th impression in 1977). This creates considerable constraints on publishers and makes the backing of innovations hazardous. The quality of a test is no guide to how widely it will be used. If reading tests have been in a backwater this cannot be entirely blamed on the test publishers.

Publishers are also constrained by the supply of new tests which actually become available for publication. Producing a new reading test from scratch can take several years and require substantial resources. One way round this has been for publishers to take advantage of development work sponsored directly or indirectly by other agencies. Many published reading tests had their development phase subsidized by a research grant from a sponsoring body. Many others were produced incidentally as part of a research or curriculum project or were developed by educational psychologists for local use. Traditionally, publishers have adopted a receptive and responsive stance, waiting for promising materials to become available rather than actively commissioning them. Certain bodies, such as the DES and NFER have initiated reading test development projects to meet currently perceived needs. As a consequence it is they, rather than publishers, who have in the past determined the kinds of tests that are developed. Publishers have acted as a filter in this process, occasionally rejecting tests as commercially unsound or, more often, influencing the format of publication; for example, by requiring shortening and simplification of materials for publication. More recently, there have been signs that some major publishers are adopting a more active policy by directly commissioning test development work, even to the extent of providing funding.

Publishers are also constrained by considerations of cost. It is understandable that schools would wish to pay as little as possible for *any* materials they use and it would be naive to expect testing to be exempt from this. However, ETSP present cases where cheapness appeared to be the *only* criterion. Their conclusions and recommendations hint that teachers should ask whether they should not be prepared to pay more for higher-quality materials and that LEAs should be prepared, also, to assist in this. If publishers are to invest in development of high quality tests they will seek a return upon this investment. Better tests will cost more. In an ideal world it would make sense to argue that the quality of evaluation and assessment should reflect the quality of the curriculum and that the balance of schools' expenditure should reflect this. A similar point applies to expenditure of resources such as time. Tests which are 'quick and simple to administer and score' are unlikely to be as informative as those which ask more of the teacher's time and effort. One would not, after all, expect a reading scheme to be cheap, simple and quick!

As far as educational tests are concerned publishers observe a more or less self-imposed code of ethics. Generally publishers do not 'push' sales of their tests and by no means supply them indiscriminately. The larger publishers restrict the supply of their reading tests to bona fide educational establishments – it is always advisable to request even inspection materials on headed school stationery. NFER-NELSON, the main source of psychological and educational tests in the UK, operates a system of grading and coding tests based on the qualifications required to use them and restricts supply accordingly.

A further feature of the publisher's role is the giving of technical advice and support in using their tests. Most publishers are only able to give very limited guidance, particularly if they handle only one or two tests. Here NFER-NELSON has a substantial advantage as it employs technically qualified staff and can call upon the expertise of NFER test developers and researchers to assist enquirers. Indeed, contact of this sort between test users and test publishers can be mutually beneficial. It is perhaps worth concluding by suggesting that users or potential users should be even more willing to liaise with publishers in this way.

CHAPTER 12

Teacher-Made Tests

It might seem incongruous that an introductory work on reading tests should include a chapter on 'do-it-yourself' test development. Various preceding chapters have implied that certain aspects of reading test production require expertise and resources beyond those a teacher is likely to possess. Someone new to reading tests might reasonably feel that it would be enough to master the use of existing materials and methods – to produce one's own versions might be seen strictly as the preserve of the advanced student of testing. It might also be pointed out that relatively few published reading tests have actually been produced by teachers working in schools – as opposed to researchers and reading specialists based outside schools.

This assumed distinction between the expertise of the teacher and that of the test producer or researcher must be questioned. This chapter will consider ways in which teachers already use expertise in testing and will suggest possibilities for further development. The discussion here may indeed stray beyond the scope of an introduction. However, there are dangers in teacher passivity: experts create tests (or techniques) for teachers to use, teachers do not take initiatives and themselves produce materials for their own use. There are many undesirable consequences to this. Not the least of these is that school-based innovations in reading curriculum would continually run ahead of test development. Existing tests would simply continue to fail to match the teaching that had taken place. In fact, there is a case for saying that teachers who wish to change or innovate must, perforce, be prepared to do more to develop means for assessing reading in the terms they have (re)conceptualized it.

Alternatives to Standardized Testing

Certain methods of assessing reading *by definition* require creative involvement of teachers who wish to use them. The IRI is perhaps the clearest example. This requires teacher-selected texts and teacher-devised questions. Published IRIs, as has been noted in Chapter 7, would not have real intrinsic advantages and could well be less appropriate in many cases. Even the related technique of miscues analysis with its apparent orthodoxies should be used flexibly according to the needs of the user.

More importantly, teacher-made approaches to assessment have a greater potential than is generally assumed for uses in areas traditionally regarded as the province of standardized testing. The necessity for a standardized norm, in particular, is often over-emphasized. For example, Stibbs (1979) discusses a case study of a Secondary English teacher who used an IRI to screen for children needing special help with reading. In this instance availability of a norm was not essential. Although it is common to employ a norm related score as a threshold criterion for screening there are many alternatives which are no more arbitrary, such as an agreed raw score, a score which places a reader in a specified lowest-scoring proportion of those screened, or signs of Frustration Level reading on a particular text. These criteria do not necessitate standardization of the instruments used.

Stibbs also suggests that an 'overview' of reading progress of a class might be assessed through fifteen minutes' observation of class reading. The teacher should watch for specific signs of difficulty and disaffection and follow the observation with a count of pages read and cloze tests based on the texts used. The session is followed up by monitoring progress with the book in the following fortnight and interviewing pupils about their reading of the book. As described, this procedure is not entirely convincing and no evidence is presented to suggest it has been tested in practice. It would also be more time-consuming than simple group testing. However, it exemplifies a method of assessment which deals in classroom realities which a teacher could more readily interpret than sets of numerical progress scores. It has the advantage of focusing more effectively on short-term progress than standardized testing does although this would not preclude its recurring use on a longitudinal basis as a means of measuring progress.

Thus screening and monitoring, two of the main uses of standardized tests, can conceivably be tackled using teacher-based alternatives. In the second example mention was made of cloze procedure. Here the distance between what teachers and test constructors can achieve is not all that great. Cloze tests have been shown to be comparable in reliability and validity to other standardized testing procedures. Much is known about how rate of deletion, grammatical class of words and sentence position, together with overall passage readability affect cloze test difficulty. These factors are discussed more fully in Rye (1982) and his guidelines can be followed as easily by teachers as by test constructors. Rye covers most of the practical details of preparing and giving cloze tests and includes a useful suggestion for grading of test difficulty by progressively increasing deletion rates. Rye also presents evidence for at least moderate validity and reliability of specific examples of teacher-made cloze tests and it would appear that with revision and retrial of materials a teacher-made test could be made as reliable as any published version. There is certainly a case for considering the use of cloze tests in monitoring and screening in school alongside other criteria suggested above. Rye also suggests cloze could contribute to grouping, ranking and comparing groups of pupils.

A further teacher-devised alternative to standardized testing in the form of checklists should be considered. *A Review of Reading Tests* draws attention to the merits of certain published examples. Their general use as an assessment device is discussed in Shipman (1983), and Stibbs (1979) makes a strong case for use of both published and teacher-made checklists in diagnosis, progress testing and preparing written assessments of children's language. To these uses might be added that of evaluation, where, as has been suggested, published materials probably make their least satisfactory contribution. Here the necessity for checklists may be simply on the grounds of economy. The range and depths of skills or activities to be assessed is too great to allow preparation of formal tests. More fundamentally, the aims of the teachers' efforts may revolve around behaviours which need observation, not testing. Take, for example, a teacher who has endeavoured to develop more effective book selection skills in a class. To test this could be an elaborate matter. It might ultimately prove much more artificial than setting a child a practical task in the school library ('Find two books which will help you in your project on . . .') and observing and checking whether the child employs the various routines and procedures she or he has been taught on a prepared checklist.

More long-term and reflective uses can also be envisaged in which a checklist is used to review, in summary, the extent to which more general aims have been achieved. This might well be appropriate where the teacher has sought to increase the extent of voluntary reading, foster interest in certain kinds of reading or develop greater autonomy in use of reference texts. The checklist could review systematically topics which were of necessity impressionistic ('Do children look for relevant books without asking for guidance?') or more concrete matters ('How many children have joined their public library?').

Towards Standardized Tests?

The problem of mismatch between test content and curriculum content was raised in an earlier paragraph. Here there will be circumstances where neither cloze procedure nor IRIs, pupil observation, checklists or interviewing will really meet the needs of evaluation. It may be that the teacher is concerned with the genuinely unassessable or it may be that relevant tests have simply not been devised. Given the limited scope of existing standardized tests the latter possibility should always be considered first! One of the criticisms that is levelled justly at some published tests is that they are out of touch with how reading is taught. For example, tests generally reflect only a partial view of reading and fail to do justice to the breadth of reading curricula to which any thoughtful teacher of reading would subscribe. It is thus insufficient to confine teacher initiatives to non-test alternatives in assessment. Nor may it be entirely necessary. Teachers spend a large part of their teaching time devising tasks and activities which in both formal and informal ways allow them to assess their teaching. It is easier to criticize tests than to devise superior alternatives but these skills are far from irrelevant in the preparation of standardized tests. In fact, teachers have by no means been excluded from standardized test development. The Edinburgh Series and *The London Reading Test* were both developed with professional participation, particularly in planning and writing the content of the tests. Similarly, APU Language Monitoring tests were evaluated prior to use by consultative groups of teachers.

Teacher involvement in test production usually stops at the point at which item-analysis trials (see Chapter 3) begin. Subsequent work tends to be carried out by specialist test constructers. If these specialists were available to conduct such work on behalf of the teachers there would be no necessity for further teacher involvement. In practice this is very rare and the absence of such experts and associated resources has precluded any independent initiatives by teachers. It is true that a number of texts on test-construction for teachers have been published. Of recent examples Satterly (1981) is the most comprehensive. However, the burden of clerical work and the problems of access to adequate samples of children for testing have usually rendered such textbook advice inert.

It would be easy to dismiss the possibility that this state of affairs could change. Continuing cuts in the funding of education could mean that teachers will have even less time for extended professional activities such as test development. Nevertheless there are some existing resources in schools and LEAs which might be adopted for development of better methods and materials for reading assessment. To start with, the computational procedures for statistical evaluation of trial versions of conventional tests are well within the scope of microcomputers of the type used in schools. Special software, although useful, is not essential. Nor do item analysis or reliability tests require results from large numbers of children. It is more important that the analysis is carried out on children who represent the range of ability for which the test is intended. It would be practical for a group of schools to pool their resources for this purpose or for an LEA advisory team to administer materials to the necessary sample. The main chore would be to record the item responses of each reader on a cassette or (preferably) disk prior to analysis. This work would probably require less time than the process of initial planning and item writing. Simple forms of validation using teachers' rankings of children or existing test results are also practicable. As we have seen in Chapter 4, really sophisticated methods of reading test validation have yet to be invented.

In this way, even a small working group of teachers could

develop a reliable and efficient test based on content which met their purposes more adequately than published materials. The establishment of test norms is a much more formidable task. It may be that the purpose of testing does not require these – it has already been suggested that both screening and progress testing are possible without norms. Grouping and curriculum planning and evaluation present a similar possibility. Before discounting the possibility of any standardization the case for preferring local to national norms should be considered. It may make more sense to scale a child's reading ability relative to some quite restricted group, such as other schools in geographical area or schools feeding the same secondary institution. The necessary cooperation for standardization on such a group is also much more easily obtained than on a national scale.

The use of a question mark in the heading of this final section has double significance. The production of teacher-made tests in the conventional format has been presented as a tentative possibility, but the question is not simply one of feasibility. There are other models of testing, particularly the diagnostic and criterion-referenced, where practitioner expertise might be better applied. Either direction of development would be even more demanding than what is suggested above. To discuss these would take the reader into the science fiction of reading testing. Yet perhaps the starting point for any creative professional initiatives in reading assessment would have to be the same thoughtful and rigorous analysis of what one means by 'reading'.

Bibliography

ANASTASI, A. (1976). *Psychological Testing.* 4th edn. New York: Macmillan.

APU (1981). *Language Performance in Schools.* Primary Survey Report No. 1. London: HMSO.

APU (1982a). *Language Performance in Schools.* Secondary Survey Report No. 1. London: HMSO.

APU (1982b). *Language Performance in Schools.* Primary Survey Report No. 2. London: HMSO.

APU (1983). *Language Performance in Schools.* Secondary Report No. 2. London: HMSO.

ARNOLD, H. (1982). *Listening to Children Reading.* London: Hodder and Stoughton.

ATHEY, L. (1978). 'A critical analysis of the Standard Reading Tests, Test 7B', *Reading,* 12, 2, 39–47.

BARNES, D. (1980). 'Situated speech strategies: aspects of monitoring oracy', *Educational Review,* 32, 2, 122–31.

BOOKBINDER, G.E. (1976). 'Reading ages and standardized scores', *Reading,* 10, 3, 20–23.

BORMUTH, J. (1968). 'Cloze test readability; criterion reference scores', *Journal of Educational Measurement,* 5, 3, 189–96.

BUROS, O.K. (1978). *Eighth Mental Measurements Yearbook.* New York: Gryphon Press.

BRIMER, A. (Ed) (1969). *Bristol Achievement Tests, English Language Levels 1 to 5.* London: Thos. Nelson.

CHAPMAN, J. (1983). *Reading Development and Cohesion.* London: Heinemann Educational Books.

CHOPPIN, B. (1979). 'Testing the questions: the Rasch model and item banking'. In: RAGGETT, M. St J., TUTT, C. and RAGGETT, P. (Eds) *Assessment and Testing of Reading*. London: Ward Lock Educational.

CLIFT, P., WEINER, G. and WILSON, E. (1981). *Record Keeping in Primary Schools*. London: Macmillan Educational Books/Schools Council.

CLYMER, T. (1972). 'What is reading? some current concepts'. In: MELNIK, A. and MERRIT, J. (Eds) *Reading Today and Tomorrow*. London: Hodder and Stoughton.

COHEN, L. (1976). *Educational Research in Classrooms and Schools: A manual of materials and methods*. London: Harper Row.

COTTERELL, G. (1973). 'Checklist of Basic Sounds'. In: COTTERELL, G. *Diagnosis in the Classroom*. Reading: Centre for the Teaching of Reading, University of Reading.

CROCKER, A.C. (1981). *Statistics for the Teacher*. 3rd edn. Windsor: NFER-NELSON.

CRONBACH, L.J. (1970). *Essentials of Psychological Measurement*. New York: Holt, Rinehard and Winston, Inc.

CRONBACH, L.J. (1971). 'Test validation'. In: THORN-DIKE, R.L. (Ed) *Educational Measurement*. Second edn. Washington: American Council on Education.

DAVIES, P. (1977). 'Language skills in sentence-level reading tests', *Reading,* 1, 27–35.

EVANS, B. and WAITES, B. (1981). *IQ and Mental Testing*. London: Macmillan.

GILLILAND, J. (1972). *Readability*. London: Hodder and Stoughton.

GIPPS, C. and WOOD, R. (1981). 'The testing of reading in LEAs: The Bullock Report seven years on', *Educational Studies,* 7, 2, 133–43.

GIPPS, C. and GOLDSTEIN, H. (1983). *Monitoring Children*. London: Heinemann Educational Books.

GIPPS, C., STEADMAN, S., BLACKSTONE, T. and STIERER, B. (1983). *Testing Children*. London: Heinemann Educational Books.

GLASER, R. (1963). 'Instructional technology and the measurement of learning outcomes: some questions', *American Psychologist,* 18, 519–21.

GOODACRE, E. (1979). 'What is reading: which model?'. In: RAGGETT, M. St J., TUTT, C. and RAGGETT, P. (Eds) *Assessment and Testing of Reading.* London: Ward Lock Educational.

GOODMAN, K.S. (1967). 'Reading: a psycholinguistic guessing game', *Journal of the Reading Specialist,* 6, 4, 12–16. Reproduced in: GOLLASCH, F.V. (Ed) (1982). *Language and Literacy: the Selected Writings of Kenneth S. Goodman, Volume 1.* Boston: Routledge and Kegan Paul.

GOODMAN, K.S. (1973). 'Miscues: a window on the reading process'. In: GOODMAN, K.S. (Ed) (1973). *Miscues Analysis: Applications to Reading Instruction.* ERIC. Reproduced in GOLLASCH, F.V. (Ed) (1982). *Language and Literacy: the Selected Writings of Kenneth S. Goodman.* Volume 1. Boston: Routledge and Kegan Paul.

GRAY, J. (1979). 'Reading progress in English infant schools: some problems emerging from a study of teacher effectiveness', *British Educational Research Journal,* 5, 2, 141–57.

GREAT BRITAIN. DEPARTMENT OF EDUCATION AND SCIENCE (1976). *Primary Education in England.* London: HMSO.

GREEN, L.F. and FRANCIS, J. (1980). 'Helping young children with special educational needs', *Remedial Education,* 15, 1, 17–22.

GREGORY, R.P., HACKNEY, C. and GREGORY, N.M. (1982). 'Corrective reading programme: an evaluation', *British Journal of Educational Psychology,* 52, 33–50.

GULLIFORD, R. (1983). 'The schools's role in assessment', *Special Education: Forward Trends,* 10, 4, 6–9.

HAMBLETON, R.K. and EIGNOR, D.R. (1978). 'Guidelines for evaluating criterion-referenced tests and test manuals', *Journal of Educational Measurement,* 15, 4, 320–7.

HARRISON, C. (1980). *Readability in the Classroom.* Cambridge: Cambridge University Press.

HOLT, M. (1981). *Evaluating the Evaluators.* Sevenoaks: Hodder and Stoughton Educational.

HUGHES, J. (1975). *Reading and Reading Failure*. London: Evans.

INGHAM, J. (1983). *The Ingham Reading Record Form*. London: Heinemann Educational Books.

JONGSMA, K.S. and JONGSMA, E.A. (1981). 'Test review: commercial informal reading inventories', *The Reading Teacher*, 34, 6, 697–704.

KAMIN, L. (1974). *The Science and Politics of IQ*. Hillsdale, New Jersey: Erlbaum.

LAWTON, D. (1980). *Politics of the School Curriculum*. London: Routledge and Kegan Paul.
LUNZER, E. and GARDNER, K. (Eds) (1979). *The Effective Use of Reading*. London: Heinemann Educational Books.

MEEK, M. (1982). *Learning to Read*. London: Bodley Head.
MILES, T.R. (1983). *Dyslexia*. St Albans: Granada Publishing.
MULLER, D.J., MUNROE, S.M. and CODE, C. (1981). *Language Assessment for Remediation*. London: Croom Helm.

NEVILLE, M.J. and PUGH, A.K. (1982). *Towards Independent Reading*. London: Heinemann Educational Books.
NITKO, A.J. (1980). 'Distinguishing the many varieties of criterion-referenced test', *Review of Educational Research*, 50, 3, 461–85.

PAVLIDES, G.T. (1979). 'How can dyslexia be objectively diagnosed?', *Reading*, 13, 3, 3–15.
PFLAUM, S.W. (1979). 'Diagnosis of oral reading', *The Reading Teacher*, 33, 3, 278–84.
POPHAM, W.J. (1978). *Criterion-Referenced Measurement*. Englewood Cliffs, New Jersey: Prentice-Hall.
POTTON, A. (1983). *Screening*. London: Macmillan Educational.
PUMFREY, P.D. and DIXON, E. (1970). 'Junior children's attitudes to reading: comments on three measuring instruments', *Reading*, 4, 2, 19–26.

PUMFREY, P.D. (1977). *Measuring Reading Abilities*. London: Hodder and Stoughton.

RABAN, B. (1983). *Reading*. London: Macmillan Educational.
RAGGET, M. St J., TUTT, C. and RAGGET, P. (Eds) (1979). *Assessment and Testing of Reading*. London: Ward Lock Educational.
ROSEN, H. (1982). *The Language Monitors*. Bedford Way Papers No. 11, Institute of Education, University of London. Redhill: TINGA TINGA (Heinemann Educational Books).
ROWNTREE, D. (1981). *Statistics Without Tears*. Harmondsworth: Penguin.
RUSSELL, J. (1970). 'Reading surveys', *Reading*, 4, 3, 13–18.
RYE, J. (1982). *Cloze Procedure and the Teaching of Reading*. London: Heinemann Educational Books.

SATTERLY, D. (1981). *Assessment in Schools*. Oxford: Basil Blackwell.
SCHELL, L.M. and HANNA, G.S. (1981). 'Can informal reading inventories reveal strengths and weaknesses in comprehension subskills?', *The Reading Teacher*, 35, 3, 263–7.
SHIPMAN, M.D. (1979). *In-School Evaluation*. London: Heinemann Educational Books.
SHIPMAN, M.D. (1983). *Assessment in Primary and Middle Schools*. London: Croom Helm.
SOUTHGATE, V., ARNOLD, A. and JOHNSON, S. (1981). *Extending Beginning Reading*. London: Heinemann Educational Books.
STIBBS, A. (1979). *Assessing Children's Language*. London: Ward Lock Educational.
STIERER, B. (1983). 'A researcher reading teachers reading children reading'. In: MEEK, M. (Ed) *Opening Moves*. Bedford Way Paper No. 17, Institute of Education, University of London. Redhill: TINGA TINGA (Heinemann Educational Books).
STOTT, D.H. (1978). *Helping Children with Learning Difficulties*. London: Ward Lock Educational.
STOTT, D.H., GREEN, L.F. and FRANCIS, J.M. (1982). *Guide to the Child's Learning Skills*. Stafford: NARE Publications.

STOTT, D.H., GREEN, L.F. and FRANCIS, J.M. (1983). 'Learning style and school attainment', *Human Learning,* 2, 61–75.

STRANG, R. (1969). *Diagnostic Teaching and Reading.* New York: McGraw-Hill.

SUMNER, R. and ROBERTSON, T.S. (1977). *Criterion-Referenced Measurement and Criterion-Referenced Tests.* Windsor: NFER.

THORNDIKE, R.L. and HAGEN, E. (1969). *Measurement and Evaluation in Psychology and Education.* New York: Wiley.

TOUGH, J. (1976). *Listening to Children Talking.* London: Ward Lock Educational for the Schools Council.

TUSON, J. and WILLMOTT, A. (1983). 'Test validity and the APU testing programme', *APU Newsletter,* No. 4, p. 7.

VINCENT, D. (1974). 'Reading ages and NFER tests', *Educational Research,* 16, 3, 176–180.

VINCENT, D. and CRESSWELL, M. (1976). *Reading Tests in the Classroom.* Windsor: NFER-NELSON.

VINCENT, D., GREEN, L., FRANCIS, J. and POWNEY, J. (1983). *A Review of Reading Tests.* Windsor: NFER-NELSON.

WALKER, C. (1974). *Reading Development and Extension.* London: Ward Lock Educational.

WILKINSON, A., STRATTA, L. and DUDLEY, P. (1974). *Schools Council Oracy Project Listening Comprehension Tests.* London: Macmillan Educational.

WILKINSON, A., BARNSLEY, G., HANNA, P. and SWAN, M. (1980). *Assessing Language Development.* Oxford: Oxford University Press.